SERV
FOR
WEEKDAYS

James Woodward
and
Leslie Houlden

For Bill Husselby
with gratitude for his vision and support
for the work of the Foundation

First published in Great Britain in 2006

Society for Promoting Christian Knowledge
36 Causton Street
London SW1P 4ST

British Library Cataloguing-in-Publication Data
A catalogue record for this book is available from the British Library

ISBN-13: 978-0-281-05760-3
ISBN-10: 0-281-05760-5

1 3 5 7 9 10 8 6 4 2

Designed and typeset by Kenneth Burnley, Wirral, Cheshire
Printed in Great Britain by Creative Print and Design

CONTENTS

Appendix

FOREWORD

Just within the borders of the Diocese of Birmingham is the Lady Katherine Leveson Foundation. Dr James Woodward is Master of the Foundation. In his time as Master, James has reminded us locally and nationally of the importance of thinking about and reflecting upon and responding to the religious needs of older people, both in our congregations and communities. This important message is one we must listen to and respond to accordingly.

This invaluable book has been written in partnership with Professor Leslie Houlden who, for many years, has worked in theological education, attempting especially to relate the New Testament to Christian discipleship. His wisdom and expertise are very evident in the compiling of this book. It will be an excellent resource for clergy and lay people who are planning short weekday services with a variety of people – for example young families and parents. In this respect, groups of older people or young parents who worship on weekdays are just as important as the Sunday congregation and deserve as much thought and preparation. In busy lives, it is not easy to do. This is where this book is so helpful in that it offers the highest possible standard of service material for any group. This is something I constantly do myself and this book will have a permanent place on my desk!

Worship is central to the Christian life and, as disciples of Jesus Christ, we should put as much energy, imagination and creativity into our worship as we can, so that we are nurtured and challenged to live the gospel.

+ Sentamu Ebor:
Archbishop of York

INTRODUCTION

The editors of this book both live in an Anglican Foundation which supports older people in community, with housing and care. James Woodward is the Master of the Foundation and Leslie Houlden a resident. Our friendship goes back to the late 1970s when the roles were somewhat reversed – Leslie Houlden was a teacher and James Woodward a student of theology at King's College, London. So this book is in part the product of many years of conversation and mutual learning as together we have grappled with the mystery of faith and its application to life. We both are enriched by each other's perspectives and learning; ready to hear the challenges and questions that ministry offers.

Each Thursday morning the community gathers to celebrate the Eucharist. This service takes place in the residents' lounge and we have a particular concern to draw in the frailer residents for worship. The service has to be short (about half an hour) and wherever possible participative. One particular difficulty that we faced was the need for us to keep the community in the rhythm of the liturgical year through the use of short Scripture readings. The three-year lectionary was difficult to use appropriately, given the range of choice and length of readings, so we devised a set of readings that was appropriate for the liturgical year.

People, both clergy and lay, who are called upon to lead worship on weekdays in groups of many kinds, often find themselves in need of aid which is not always readily forthcoming. Sometimes they operate at short notice; sometimes they find no ready source of assistance with readings, addresses or prayers; sometimes they need a prompt in the wings.

This book offers, for each week and major occasion of the year, a brief and accessible Scripture reading, almost always from the New Testament and mostly from the Gospels. Then we give two comments on each passage: first a succinct exegetical comment, then a more discursive and personal reflection. Both set out to help people as they consider what to say in an address. In our worship here we have found it helpful to open up a conversation about the biblical passage by asking a question concerning either our faith or our life experience. What has emerged has challenged some of our perceptions about how people learn about faith and what rich and wonderful lives we human beings share. We have also learnt about the particular spiritual wisdom that old age can bring. We have been surprised by the creative way in which people have engaged with Scripture and how appreciative they have been to have been given a voice: 'The sermon becomes ours and not just yours,' exclaims a resident!

The final section offers brief bullet points to stimulate prayer and further reflection. In all this we have attempted to engage the reader in a deeper attention to the word of God and its power to illuminate the path of our journey.

In the compiling of this book we have embraced the possibility of its being of wider use to both individuals and groups. It may be of use to those churches which have weekday services for other groups such as young families. It may also be of use to individuals to enrich their devotional life. With this wider audience in mind we have offered a range of styles and approaches in the Reflection section in the hope that it offers a starting point for enriching the Christian year.

Our thanks to the community of the Foundation of Lady Katherine Leveson and especially those faithful women and men who listen and pray and whose reflections have shaped this book. Thanks also to Jenny Jones for her willing secretarial support. For more information about the Foundation please visit our website: <www.leveson.org.uk>. The authors can be contacted via e-mail at <templehouse@btinternet.com>.

James Woodward
Leslie Houlden

THE SERVICES

ADVENT 1

ISAIAH 9.2, 6, 7

The people who walked in darkness have seen a great light; those who lived in a land of deep darkness – on them light has shined.

For a child has been born for us, a son given to us; authority rests upon his shoulders; and he is named Wonderful Counsellor, Mighty God, Everlasting Father, Prince of Peace.

His authority shall grow continually, and there shall be endless peace for the throne of David and his kingdom. He will establish and uphold it with justice and with righteousness from this time onwards and for evermore.

*The zeal of the L*ORD *of hosts will do this.*

COMMENTARY

Advent is the great time to nourish Christian eagerness – for the richness of God's love and the peace of his presence. The prophet Isaiah fixes his hope on a royal child. Such a birth is always a time for expectation of better times. No wonder Christians have always read these words as pointing to Jesus; and especially the focus is on his appearing – and so too on Christmas. But yet there is more, even beyond that. How far can a Christian's hope stretch? To the end of our lives and the aims we still have in our hearts? To the end of the world we know? Such things are beyond our reach; but we can always hope for what is good and fine – and to know God.

REFLECTION

Advent leads us into a waiting mode of living. Children are caught up in the excitement of waiting for Christmas. The experience of waiting is a common one and it shapes the rhythm of our lives. We wait for trains, for the post or for pay-day. Perhaps when we think of Jesus we think of him waiting, of him trusting, of him being open and vulnerable and exposed. Jesus discloses in his waiting the deepest dimensions of the glory of God – as he waits in exposure and helplessness for what is to come.

Although this experience of waiting is a common one, we live in a world where we want or create a culture within which waiting is undesirable. We live in a world where we are promised that we can have what we want and have it *now* – and more than that, that we can have *now* what we do not want or need.

Jesus shows us that waiting has its own value and dignity. Advent is the invitation to wait with hope for the future that is to come. God's future is not an invitation that we find easy to accept. We live in a time when thoughts of the future may fill people with fear and not with hope and joy. We must learn to hope, to rest, to pray, and to wait.

- Let us think about waiting and God's future promise as we prepare for Christmas.

- Pray to open up yourself to God, ready to trust and to hope.

- Pray for those who wait, especially those in the vulnerable situations of weakness or illness.

ADVENT 2

LUKE 19.41-44

As Jesus came near and saw the city, he wept over it, saying, 'If you, even you, had only recognized on this day the things that make for peace! But now they are hidden from your eyes.

'Indeed the days will come upon you, when your enemies will set up ramparts around you and surround you, and hem you in on every side.

'They will crush you to the ground, you and your children within you, and they will not leave within you one stone upon another; because you did not recognize the time of your visitation from God.'

COMMENTARY

People reading this passage nowadays (and often in the past) cannot help seeing it as pointing to the events in Jerusalem with which we are all too familiar – shootings and bombings and sudden death. Jesus' words were vividly fulfilled only 40 years after his time, when a Roman army destroyed the city, including the Temple itself. But the words go deeper than a news report in advance. They are chiefly a lament for the way our failure to see God's love for us carries with it all kinds of disaster. People often see this as God's punishment: but do we not bring it on ourselves when we fail to see what God puts before our eyes?

REFLECTION

Every year at this time I send out a Christmas card to every house in the parish. With it I try to articulate something of the meaning and power of the Christmas story of God's visitation of love. However, in any attempt to articulate the happiness and light that Christmas brings, one is constantly brought up sharp against the deeper darkness of our world and human nature. The angels proclaim 'Peace in heaven and glory on high', but we continue to live in a world torn apart by evidence of the blindness and destructiveness of the human will. So there is a dramatic tension between our lives as God would have them to be and the realities of how we live them. God's will for peace, joy and reconciliation

4

comes up against the gloom of people who reject the joy, and the blindness of men and women who drift into disastrous conflicts and wars.

In this passage no resolution of the tears is offered. We are brought face to face with our human weakness and the sheer fragility of the world and its history.

Our laments and indeed our tears are a precious part of the human response to the paradoxes and contradictions which shape all our lives. We should be wary of over-easy or triumphalist answers. We should keep on articulating the unanswered questions which cause us pain. Above all, at a human level, we should keep on crying for those things in life which perplex and distress us. Our task in making the Christmas story of love real is to hold together tensions between the idealism of love and the reality of how we fail to be what God wills for us.

- When you look at the world around you, what are the things that cause you to weep?
- Pray for peace in your own heart and in the troubled hearts of our world.
- Ask for God's blessing and grace on the questions you ask about Christian living and its contradictions.

ADVENT 3

MATTHEW 11.2–6

When John heard in prison what the Messiah was doing, he sent word by his disciples and said to Jesus, 'Are you the one who is to come, or are we to wait for another?'

Jesus answered them, 'Go and tell John what you hear and see: the blind receive their sight, the lame walk, the lepers are cleansed, the deaf hear, the dead are raised, and the poor have good news brought to them.

'And blessed is anyone who takes no offence at me.'

COMMENTARY

The question is: what is the meaning of Jesus' healings and other great good deeds? Well, they are certainly acts of pity for sufferers. But they go further. They point to the deeper meaning of Jesus' mission – to the kingdom of God. His acts are small-scale signs of God's love – little signals of how things ought to be. It is work that in all kinds of ways Christians have continued from that day to this. And God's love is made visible in the midst of our lives.

REFLECTION

Fear is one of the most controlling emotions in our lives. Perhaps most of us do not like to think of ourselves as fearful people – we prefer to imagine ourselves as strong, energetic and independent. The world is full of fears – and we all, at some point or other, have felt afraid, frozen and gripped by fear.

John the Baptist was afraid: in a cold, dark prison, alone and unaware of what might happen next. In the prison of his doubts and fears, John looks to Christ; he looks to the one who is free and asks, 'Who are you?'

The reply from Jesus is significant. He points beyond himself to God and proclaims: 'Look at what God is doing through me!' In Christ a new regime is ushered in, a world of healing and liberation, which the company of those who believe him can see. Jesus embodies the healing presence of God.

In this third week of Advent, it is time for us to consider our lives and to acknowledge our fears. Of what are we afraid? What are the fears which imprison us? What are the fears that imprison the Church, our community, the world? Let us pray for light to see that which imprisons us and for grace to ask from our prisons, with John the Baptist, the same question of Jesus: 'Are you the one who is to come?'

- Let us affirm and celebrate Christ's healing and liberation, and his visionary gospel at work today.

- Pray for that gospel to work in your own life to free you from your own imprisonments and blindness.

- Let us pray that we may see the goodness of Jesus present among us in this act of worship.

ADVENT 4

LUKE 1.46–55

And Mary said, 'My soul magnifies the Lord, and my spirit rejoices in God my Saviour, for he has looked with favour on the lowliness of his servant.

'Surely, from now on all generations will call me blessed; for the Mighty One has done great things for me, and holy is his name.

'His mercy is for those who fear him from generation to generation. He has shown strength with his arm; he has scattered the proud in the thoughts of their hearts.

'He has brought down the powerful from their thrones, and lifted up the lowly; he has filled the hungry with good things, and sent the rich away empty.

'He has helped his servant Israel, in remembrance of his mercy, according to the promise he made to our ancestors, to Abraham and to his descendants for ever.'

COMMENTARY

Mary's song, the *Magnificat*, comes frequently in Christian worship, but it began as a hymn of praise, even ecstasy, offered to God for the wonder of Jesus' coming. Mary sees him as turning the world upside down. It is strange that our religion has often seemed to be on the side of things as they are. Mary does not see it like that at all. Jesus will alter everything: uproot the rich and powerful, and promote the poor and weak. It is a wonderful picture – enough to frighten and excite us at the same time. Can we bear the truth of God's purposes?

REFLECTION

St Luke tells us that Mary treasures and ponders all these things in her heart. She is in some way the memory of the Church, its inner sanctuary where the most intimate secrets of God's dealings with his people are pondered and treasured.

I have come to know the spiritual reality of Mary with the Sisters of the Love of God, an Anglican community whose vocation is that of prayer, silence and contemplation. Perhaps the Church in its wisest moments has seen that the mysteries of Mary are somehow hidden inner mysteries, to be pondered and discerned in prayer and silence and not to be proclaimed from the rooftops.

That constant pondering and treasuring of the things of God remain at the heart of God's people through the centuries of the history of the Church. We are calling people to be with God through service and worship, through prayer and struggle. We must discern the way into which we are being guided, amidst hesitations and uncertainties, so that we can enlarge and deepen the holiness, the catholicity and the sheer wondrous beauty of God.

We are living through times of change and controversy, but there is a call to us to treasure and ponder in our hearts all those inner riches that God has granted to his people in the centuries of Christian history.

- Pray that we may enter into the silence and faithfulness of Mary.
- Pray that we may share more fully her response of obedience and love.
- May the new come to birth in us as it came to birth in her.

CHRISTMAS

LUKE 2.8–15

In that region there were shepherds living in the fields, keeping watch over their flock by night. Then an angel of the Lord stood before them, and the glory of the Lord shone around them, and they were terrified.

But the angel said to them, 'Do not be afraid; for see – I am bringing you good news of great joy for all the people: to you is born this day in the city of David a Saviour, who is the Messiah, the Lord. This will be a sign for you: you will find a child wrapped in bands of cloth and lying in a manger.'

And suddenly there was with the angel a multitude of the heavenly host, praising God and saying, 'Glory to God in the highest heaven, and on earth peace among those whom he favours!'

When the angels had left them and gone into heaven, the shepherds said to one another, 'Let us go now to Bethlehem and see this thing that has taken place, which the Lord has made known to us.'

COMMENTARY

Shepherds are the first people to hear of the birth of Jesus. People who followed this occupation were seen as not acceptable by 'proper' Jews of the time – their work made it unlikely that they could fulfil their religious duties. So right at the start, those on the margins receive the good news. Luke's Gospel emphasizes this as the heart of Jesus' mission from start to finish. But the message is given by an angel, and then the scene is filled with angels. In other words, the saving message comes with the most striking show of God's reality and power. And so we see the two-fold response: honour to God and wholesome renewal to those who receive the amazing gift.

REFLECTION

The Christmas stories are centred on a number of journeys. This includes the journey of the shepherds to see the great things that have happened

– a journey made in surprise and hope, and ending in wonderment. We too make our own journeys in life. Sometimes we spend a great deal of our time looking backwards or forwards. But there are dangers in these journeys – nostalgia, optimism and naïvety. The search for something real or imagined can be fantasy and escape.

Perhaps part of the attraction of Christmas is the search for lost innocence. As we look at the shepherds gazing on the baby, it is the innocence of Christmas which grips our heart, the innocence of the Virgin and child which both convicts and uplifts us.

Yet innocence is not a quality by which today's world sets much store. The search for lost innocence can easily begin to seem a misguided or hopeless dream. Innocence offers us a purity of heart which sees God in everything, and this seems a hopeless dream in our world of self-interested calculation and studied effect. But innocence leads us to see the best in people, however hard it may be.

The Christmas message is that such burning and shining innocence is not a dream or a delusion. It has been made actual and real for us in the life of Jesus. Let us with the shepherds take a journey of the heart, to Bethlehem, that we may find the source of innocence, the God of love. And in worship, we shall taste its reality.

- Thank God for the innocence of the childlike response to Christmas love.

- Pray for all those who will worship this Christmas.

- Reflect further on the various journeys and characters that make up our Christmas story.

CHRISTMAS 1

JOHN 1.1–9, 14

In the beginning was the Word, and the Word was with God, and the Word was God. He was in the beginning with God.

All things came into being through him, and without him not one thing came into being.

What has come into being in him was life, and the life was the light of all people. The light shines in the darkness, and the darkness did not overcome it.

There was a man sent from God, whose name was John. He came as a witness to testify to the light, so that all might believe through him. He himself was not the light, but he came to testify to the light.

The true light, which enlightens everyone, was coming into the world . . . And the Word became flesh and lived among us, and we have seen his glory, the glory as of a father's only son, full of grace and truth.

COMMENTARY

John echoes the story of creation in Genesis 1. Like a powerful ruler who speaks and whose orders are obeyed, so God speaks and things come into being – first light, then on and on, climaxing in human beings. So the coming of Jesus is a kind of new creation, a whole new start. Only Jesus sums up and gives newness to everything: he is 'light' and 'life' and indeed a new start for the human race – and all in accordance with God's mind, expressing itself in all things. So God's 'Word' and 'light' and 'life' come together before our eyes in Jesus, the 'Word made flesh', God putting himself in our midst, as one of us.

REFLECTION

There is a restaurant in the Musée D'Orsay in Paris called the Clock Tower. Here you can sit and watch the world go by through the clear glass of the clock face. The hands of the clock (about 12 feet long) mark the time. Through this clock face you get a wonderful view of the life of Paris – a world busying itself in time.

The image has the power to reflect something of the message of Christmas. God sees through time. God is beyond time. Before time God was and is. When time ends God will still be. God is all-powerful – mysterious, full of grandeur and majesty and glory. And our perceptions are partial and limited. God – the source of all being – is not limited either by us or by the ticking of any clock.

This God who is beyond time speaks to us in time. This God knows us and loves us and will never let us go. This God shows us his love by coming to us in time – through the particularity of a person in history, Jesus Christ. This God addresses us in all the details of our lives with all the earthed practical wisdom that can give us direction, depth and purpose. This is a love that is with us and for us, and can lift our horizons to inspire us. A God beyond time but within it – a God that has the power to change us and transform us. May that love and the God beyond but within time be in our hearts and lives this Christmas.

- Pray for a wise use of time.

- Thank God for the limitations and the opportunities of time.

- Thank God for the way in which he speaks to us in history and in time.

EPIPHANY

MATTHEW 2.1–12

In the time of King Herod, after Jesus was born in Bethlehem of Judea, wise men from the East came to Jerusalem, asking, 'Where is the child who has been born king of the Jews? For we observed his star at its rising, and have come to pay him homage.'

When King Herod heard this, he was frightened, and all Jerusalem with him; and calling together all the chief priests and scribes of the people, he inquired of them where the Messiah was to be born.

They told him, 'In Bethlehem of Judea; for so it has been written by the prophet: "And you, Bethlehem, in the land of Judah, are by no means least among the rulers of Judah; for from you shall come a ruler who is to shepherd my people Israel."'

Then Herod secretly called for the wise men and learned from them the exact time when the star had appeared. Then he sent them to Bethlehem, saying, 'Go and search diligently for the child; and when you have found him, bring me word so that I may also go and pay him homage.'

When they had heard the king, they set out; and there, ahead of them, went the star that they had seen at its rising, until it stopped over the place where the child was. When they saw that the star had stopped, they were overwhelmed with joy.

On entering the house, they saw the child with Mary his mother; and they knelt down and paid him homage. Then, opening their treasure-chests, they offered him gifts of gold, frankincense, and myrrh.

And having been warned in a dream not to return to Herod, they left for their own country by another road.

COMMENTARY

The 'wise men' are astrologers, the clever intellectuals of their day – and they are foreigners, so they have the mystery and fascination of the exotic. How wonderful that such people (think of top American scientists) come to the infant Jesus, having taken great trouble. Clever Gentiles contrast with the king of the Jewish realm – and the future lies with the former: Matthew's Gospel ends with the prospect of Jesus' leading followers 'making disciples of all nations'. The mission of Jesus is without limit. The symbolic gifts which the magi bring stand for aspects of Jesus' future role (rule, worship and death). They draw on old scriptural associations – as does the later thought that the visitors were 'three kings': see Isaiah 60.1–6 and Psalm 72. The idea that there were *three* wise men comes simply from there being three gifts. More important, these great figures actually venerate the child Jesus.

REFLECTION

Three aspects of this story as told by Matthew might help us to connect it with our own lives. The first is that the wise men saw the star when they were busy with their ordinary tasks and work. The revelation of God can be found when we are busy with the ordinary things of our lives – God speaks to us in all kinds of ways: while washing up; in the smile of a child; in our concern for others. We then might attend more to the ordinariness of life and glimpse in and through our attention the presence of God.

Second, it took outsiders to point to a great fact: the significance of the baby Jesus. Are we today prepared to allow others to speak to us and to show us how to change and grow?

Third, they gave their gifts in an act of worship. Gifts of charity can sometimes do more harm than good. We must look at our motivations and if we are to give, then let us do it out of love. The wise men offer us an example of giving – they gave to the newborn King with love and in reverent and humble generosity. We must yield to him out of love. By his love we can be set free to love and be loved. The gift of gold symbolizes the substance of God; frankincense symbolizes our inner treasure of thought and influence, and myrrh is symbolic of our vulnerability to be used for and by God.

- Thank God for the ways in which his generous love is revealed.
- Reflect on your own giving.
- Pray for your work.

BAPTISM OF CHRIST

MARK 1.1–11

The beginning of the good news of Jesus Christ, the Son of God. As it is written in the prophet Isaiah, 'See, I am sending my messenger ahead of you, who will prepare your way; the voice of one crying out in the wilderness: "Prepare the way of the Lord, make his paths straight".'

John the baptizer appeared in the wilderness, proclaiming a baptism of repentance for the forgiveness of sins. And people from the whole Judean countryside and all the people of Jerusalem were going out to him, and were baptized by him in the river Jordan, confessing their sins.

Now John was clothed with camel's hair, with a leather belt around his waist, and he ate locusts and wild honey. He proclaimed, 'The one who is more powerful than I is coming after me; I am not worthy to stoop down and untie the thong of his sandals. I have baptized you with water; but he will baptize you with the Holy Spirit.'

In those days Jesus came from Nazareth of Galilee and was baptized by John in the Jordan. And just as he was coming up out of the water, he saw the heavens torn apart and the Spirit descending like a dove on him. And a voice came from heaven, 'You are my Son, the Beloved; with you I am well pleased.'

COMMENTARY

This is the opening of the Gospel of Mark, the first of the four to be written. For Mark, John the Baptist is simply the 'herald', announcing Jesus' coming and making his identity plain. So John is the final prophet – and he bears the marks of Elijah, the greatest prophet of Israel whose return was foretold by Malachi as the herald of God's great Messiah. We notice the repeated use of 'way' in the opening quotes from scriptural prophecy: all through this Gospel Mark sees Jesus' life and death as the journey he must make, bringing God's purposes to their fulfilment (see 10.32–34, 46, 52). Then comes the dramatic act of baptism. It is God's commissioning of Jesus for his role as God's chosen agent (see Psalm 2.7 for background).

REFLECTION

Water is for us an ambivalent thing. Our ancestors came out of it, yet it is the element in which we are never truly at home. Without it we cannot live, within it we cannot live either. It is both the river of life and the cruel sea. And going down to the waters in a ritual total immersion is a symbol not only of cleansing but of that last and total surrender which is death. By the same token, the coming up out of the water is a sign of re-birth, of resurrection to victorious life. By submitting his Son to this act of baptism at the very beginning of his public ministry, God the Father sets forth a pattern of our Lord's work of salvation: life achieved by the offering of himself in death.

As we say the 'Our Father' we come to be alongside Jesus. That means Jesus as we have seen him in his baptism. We come first in the humility of our mere human condition, without pretensions of culture or learning or wealth or social status, of Church or race, without even pretensions to righteousness. And second we come ready to find true life in Jesus' own way – through death: death to egotism, self-interest, self-indulgence, self-concern; death, if need be, prematurely and voluntarily to earthly life itself.

- Give thanks for your own baptism.
- Pray for a deepening of the spirit of human unity.
- Pray to see the glory of God in the mere humanity of every man, woman and child.

EPIPHANY 2

LUKE 2.41–52

Now every year Jesus' parents went to Jerusalem for the festival of the Passover. And when he was twelve years old, they went up as usual for the festival.

When the festival was ended and they started to return, the boy Jesus stayed behind in Jerusalem, but his parents did not know it. Assuming that he was in the group of travellers, they went a day's journey.

Then they started to look for him among their relatives and friends. When they did not find him, they returned to Jerusalem to search for him.

After three days they found him in the temple, sitting among the teachers, listening to them and asking them questions. And all who heard him were amazed at his understanding and his answers.

When his parents saw him they were astonished; and his mother said to him, 'Child, why have you treated us like this? Look, your father and I have been searching for you in great anxiety.'

He said to them, 'Why were you searching for me? Did you not know that I must be in my Father's house?' But they did not understand what he said to them.

Then he went down with them and came to Nazareth, and was obedient to them. His mother treasured all these things in her heart. And Jesus increased in wisdom and in years, and in divine and human favour.

COMMENTARY

This is the only story about Jesus' childhood anywhere in the Gospels. At the age of 12 he is taken to Jerusalem for Passover for the first time. For the reader of the whole story of Jesus, it is natural to think ahead to the later Passover when his mission would reach its climax. This time, however, the focus is first on Jesus' independence – he has his own role to pursue – and then on his humble apprenticeship: even Jesus, among us and one of us, must learn the teaching handed down by the leaders of Israel. Not surprisingly, he was a 'wonder child', absorbing all that was passed before him. Jesus will bring many new things, but he does not abandon his God-given heritage.

REFLECTION

Every Thursday morning in school term time our church is filled with children from the church school who come for their weekly act of worship. They come open and ready to both sing and pray. They come ready to lay before God their hopes and fears and learn more of his gospel of grace. They listen and respond. In these respects they replicate Jesus' listening witness. We have much to learn here.

There is another aspect of this story that needs to stay with us. Jesus' complete commitment to the ways of his Father is the bedrock of his life story. He is about to embark on this life, and he announces his openness to God. His trust, his desire to learn more, his openness and depth challenge us to re-focus our allegiance on the wisdom and life-changing truth of God.

- Give thanks for the ways in which children teach us to learn more about the spiritual.

- Pray for all parents as they guide their families.

- Pray for a deeper thirst for a knowledge of God.

EPIPHANY 3

ACTS 9.1–9

Saul, still breathing threats and murder against the disciples of the Lord, went to the high priest and asked him for letters to the synagogues at Damascus, so that if he found any who belonged to the Way, men or women, he might bring them bound to Jerusalem.

Now as he was going along and approaching Damascus, suddenly a light from heaven flashed around him. He fell to the ground and heard a voice saying to him, 'Saul, Saul, why do you persecute me?'

He asked, 'Who are you, Lord?' The reply came, 'I am Jesus, whom you are persecuting. But get up and enter the city, and you will be told what you are to do.'

The men who were travelling with him stood speechless because they heard the voice but saw no one. Saul got up from the ground, and though his eyes were open, he could see nothing; so they led him by the hand and brought him into Damascus. For three days he was without sight, and neither ate nor drank.

COMMENTARY

Until we reach Gentile lands, Luke, in writing Acts, uses for Paul his Jewish name, Saul (in this and other ways, Luke is sensitive to the changing setting of his story). The story of his conversion to his new role as the 'apostle' or agent of Jesus is described briefly in the first chapter of Paul's own letter to his converts in Galatia (in modern Turkey); but Luke tells the story in detail, and it is one of the most significant events in the early days of Christianity. First, because Paul was the first great effective missionary, taking the message of salvation through Jesus to many cities in Turkey and Greece; second, because he was the first to see that Jesus' coming was for everybody, not Jews alone – and this must mean not insisting that non-Jews take on becoming Jews as part of the process of following Jesus. No, Jesus was the direct route to God for *all*. Paul was revolutionary!

REFLECTION

Art can help us to see life afresh and reflect upon it, through colour, movement, light and darkness. And in our seeing we can help others to see.

Saul, blinded by his spiritual awakening, saw in the wonderful light of that crippling blindness who Jesus was in the mysterious plan of the Father, revealed as the eternal means to reconcile all things with himself. In the Cross and Resurrection he saw the judgement and the restoration of the whole creation. This is the gospel that Paul lived by and died for: a vision of how reality truly is, the love and sacrifice that create, redeem and reconcile. In the light of Christ we see all things as they are, in their particular beauty, or with the compassion which God himself has for the suffering or the sinful.

- Give thanks for the ministry of Paul and his letters of encouragement and challenge.

- Pray for the grace to see the mystery of God's presence in change.

- Ask for God's blessing on the mission of the Church.

EPIPHANY 4

LUKE 2.27–32

Guided by the Spirit, Simeon came into the temple; and when the parents brought in the child Jesus, to do for him what was customary under the law, Simeon took him in his arms and praised God, saying, 'Master, now you are dismissing your servant in peace, according to your word; for my eyes have seen your salvation, which you have prepared in the presence of all peoples, a light for revelation to the Gentiles and for glory to your people Israel.'

COMMENTARY

The opening chapters of Luke's Gospel keep returning to the Jerusalem Temple. It is as if he wants to insist that we do not lose sight of the roots of Jesus (and of his work) in Israel, its scriptures and institutions. We all get our significance in part from our roots; and Luke sees Jesus' roots as given by God. So Simeon represents the best in old Israel and voices its mission and its hopes, now concentrated in the figure of the infant Jesus. His role is universal, going beyond the bounds of Israel to the whole human race. No wonder that the passage is linked with a festival of light, Candlemas, on 2 February.

REFLECTION

'Revelation' can sometimes have negative associations, when it is the unveiling of that which wishes to remain hidden – whether for good reasons or bad. Our 'revelations', so called, can cause havoc and distress, or simply mislead us.

But here Simeon acknowledges the true revelation, an unveiling which enlightens, an uncovering which is freely made, and which requires a free and honest response without manipulation. This is a communication which creates light, which reaches out in love. The word is spoken to bring an end to division, spoken with respect – God's salvation is openly shown to all in Jesus.

For Simeon, seeing all the fullness of God in the face of the child was the culmination of his own life of faithfulness and waiting, and brought it to a conclusion. Simeon's song, the *Nunc dimittis*, is often therefore used at funerals – a prayer offered to the eternal God on behalf of a soul.

- Give thanks for the glimpses of God's light in your community.

- Pray for all older people and the wisdom that their experience has given to the world.

- Pray for an uncovering of the knowledge of God's truth to guide you through life towards death.

EPIPHANY 5

LUKE 12.13–21

Someone in the crowd said to Jesus, 'Teacher, tell my brother to divide the family inheritance with me.' But he said to him, 'Friend, who set me to be a judge or arbitrator over you?'

And he said to them, 'Take care! Be on your guard against all kinds of greed; for one's life does not consist in the abundance of possessions.'

Then he told them a parable: 'The land of a rich man produced abundantly. And he thought to himself, "What should I do, for I have no place to store my crops?" Then he said, "I will do this: I will pull down my barns and build larger ones, and there I will store all my grain and my goods. And I will say to my soul, Soul, you have ample goods laid up for many years; relax, eat, drink, be merry."

'But God said to him, "You fool! This very night your life is being demanded of you. And the things you have prepared, whose will they be?" So it is with those who store up treasures for themselves but are not rich towards God.'

COMMENTARY

No reader of Luke's Gospel could fail to see that Jesus was firm about the moral and spiritual dangers of being rich. Time and again, Jesus' teaching is as clear on the subject as could be; and the modern Christian reader who finds it uncomfortable has no grounds for wriggling out of the challenge. We should of course note differences between his society and ours. Most obviously, there was nothing to correspond to our welfare state in the world of Jesus, and there was little to curb the ambitions of those on the make. In some ways, we may feel that little has changed in either respect in many modern societies, but at least some countries have safety nets, even if there is plenty of scope for greed. But Jesus' objection to wealth is less a matter of social or political policy (he blesses the condition of the poor!) than of the sense of dependence on God which riches muffle. There is little more likely to stifle our love for God than the contentment with self that wealth can breed.

REFLECTION

'I never inherited my money – I earned it through hard work' was a heartfelt and honest response by a parishioner to a sermon on the dangers of wealth. No doubt wealth was important for him because it gave him some control over the future and some security.

However, control over life is largely illusory, as we can see from the way that many people acquire their wealth. Sometimes there just happens to be a good harvest. So to some extent we ourselves make our lives, but only on the basis of what is given to us: what we owe to family, friends, circumstance, events which simply happen to us. The writing of the stories of our lives is done only a little by ourselves, mostly by other people, by what happens to us, but ultimately by God. Alas, it is the affluent who most easily forget this. People on the edge of destitution are naturally aware of how dependent they are on what happens to them. But the seduction of wealth is the illusion it gives us of control over our lives.

So we must be very wary of all attempts to imagine that it is only we who write the story, and we must beware of the dangers that wealth brings to the shape of our lives.

- Pray for the poor.
- How do you use your money?
- Pray for the things or people that control your life.

EPIPHANY 6

ACTS 4.32–37

Now the whole group of those who believed were of one heart and soul, and no one claimed private ownership of any possessions, but everything they owned was held in common. With great power the apostles gave their testimony to the resurrection of the Lord Jesus, and great grace was upon them all.

There was not a needy person among them, for as many as owned lands or houses sold them and brought the proceeds of what was sold. They laid it at the apostles' feet, and it was distributed to each as any had need.

There was a Levite, a native of Cyprus, Joseph, to whom the apostles gave the name Barnabas (which means 'son of encouragement'). He sold a field that belonged to him, then brought the money and laid it at the apostles' feet.

COMMENTARY

This passage, from the early chapters of the Acts of the Apostles, gives us a rare glimpse of life in the earliest Christian community in Jerusalem. Luke, the author of Acts, clearly sees this first church after Jesus' resurrection and ascension as a model for how the Christian groups ought to arrange their affairs. In effect, they are to live as if they were a single household, pooling their resources (and of course providing for the poorer members). It is an idyllic picture: was it already a fond memory when Luke was writing (perhaps 60 years later) and is he in part hoping to prick the consciences of his readers? And once more, what you do with your property and how attached you are to it is a major measure of the state of your soul.

REFLECTION

Resources are gifts to share, not to shield. All of us need to overcome the road-block of indulgence – focusing solely on self where the soul becomes fatter and lazier. Too much intake and not enough activity makes us spiritually obese in our caring. The regular sharing of who we are and what we possess expresses our regard and love for one another. So we need to be challenged by this passage in asking ourselves how we respond to each other with gracious, Christ-like compassion. What are the limitations that we place upon our desire to care for others? Where are the boundaries of our love?

This is radical stuff because it tells us that resources are gifts to steward, not to stockpile. So many of us are overcome with a hoarding spirit – marked by greed, bitterness, loneliness and insecurity. Is it possible to learn to release our possessions by not holding them so tightly? How might our lives best express this spirit of openness and freedom which can create sustainable and generous hearts and communities? It is time to look again at how we use our resources and what we give away.

- Reflect on your attitude to possessions.
- Pray for a deepening of a generous spirit.
- Reflect on those individuals in need in your community.

EPIPHANY 7

LUKE 4.16–21

When he came to Nazareth, where he had been brought up, Jesus went to the synagogue on the sabbath day, as was his custom.

He stood up to read, and the scroll of the prophet Isaiah was given to him. He unrolled the scroll and found the place where it was written:

'The Spirit of the Lord is upon me, because he has anointed me to bring good news to the poor. He has sent me to proclaim release to the captives and recovery of sight to the blind, to let the oppressed go free, to proclaim the year of the Lord's favour.'

And he rolled up the scroll, gave it back to the attendant, and sat down. The eyes of all in the synagogue were fixed on him. Then he began to say to them, 'Today this scripture has been fulfilled in your hearing.'

COMMENTARY

Luke took this story of Jesus revisiting his home town and its synagogue from the Gospel of Mark (6.1–6), but he gave it a more prominent position: it comes right at the start of Jesus' public ministry. And he tells us that Jesus read from a scroll in the synagogue. He chose the opening of Isaiah 61, with its marvellous picture of God's purpose for human liberation. The effect is stunning. The words act as a kind of keynote speech for Jesus' ministry as a whole. We now know what his policy will be, and the rest of the book, right to the Cross itself, will simply work it out. Who says religion and politics must not mix!

REFLECTION

In our lives it is always difficult to achieve a balance between empathy and confrontation. We long to be understood and we all need to be listened to. However, there are always times when what we have done or said or how we construct our sense of ourselves in the world needs challenging and perhaps changing. Our ability to comprehend and to understand are limited, and so for growth we need to be listened to and also challenged. In other words, we need both stability and insecurity if we are to be able to grow deeply into a mature sense of ourselves and our destiny.

The Church needs changing too and it needs its prophets and prophecies. The ministry of Jesus is prophetic – it will challenge and change the worlds of those who attend to its message. This prophecy brings love and consolation but also judgement. Jesus uses the language of liberation and we would do well to hear again the urgency and the daring of this call – to be shaken out of our complacency and to be confronted by the radical inclusion articulated here. This prophetic call stamps upon us all a call to social action and social justice; a concern for the inclusion of the poor, the blind and the oppressed. We must always look outside our own circle to others and their place within the Kingdom.

- Pray for those that society excludes for whatever reason.
- Pray to be liberated from self-concern and complacency.
- Pray for all those individuals and groups involved in social action for justice.

SECOND SUNDAY BEFORE LENT

MATTHEW 7.1-5

'Do not judge, so that you may not be judged. For with the judgement you make you will be judged, and the measure you give will be the measure you get.

'Why do you see the speck in your neighbour's eye, but do not notice the log in your own eye? Or how can you say to your neighbour, "Let me take the speck out of your eye", while the log is in your own eye?

'You hypocrite, first take the log out of your own eye, and then you will see clearly to take the speck out of your neighbour's eye.'

COMMENTARY

Nobody would like to think him/herself a nonentity, counting for nothing. And being 'somebody' means having opinions about all kinds of things that matter to us – and about the people that come our way. Does that not mean that we cannot help 'judging' others? And if that means that we are judged by others, it is surely part of the deal – though we may prefer not to know what their judgement is. It seems to be an inevitable part of life that we all constantly form opinions about one another – in effect 'judge' them, and sometimes with important consequences (for example, if we have the task of selecting people for jobs). So how can we deal with this teaching of Jesus – which at first sight looks fair and good for our souls but on second thoughts seems almost impossible, even undesirable! Well, let us make sure that we never suppose for one moment that we ourselves are immune: as we judge, form opinions about others, let us always remember that we too are fallible and sinful creatures of the one God who creates and loves us all for his good ends.

REFLECTION

One of the times I have been brought up sharp with my own judgementalism was during a dinner party when I was talking about a university contemporary of mine known to the host. As I finished my rather sharp judgement of the individual, the host asked, 'And tell us now what do you think they would say about you and your time at college?' It was right to be reminded of the ways in which we constantly criticize and judge. There is something of the hypocrite in us all.

I took that challenge away and reflected upon the dangers of being a judge. We need to be careful about our excessively sharp eyes. Moreover there is self-indulgence in us all as we seek out the faults in others. It is an expression of the dullness of our vision as we stand in front of our mirrors.

But we also need help in generating constructive attitudes for assessing both ourselves and others. We are reminded that we should be gracious, merciful and patient. These are virtues that can be nurtured. Further, we should practise self-examination – an honesty which can see with love from the heart. Finally, in the uncomfortable and disturbing words of the Gospel of Matthew, we should see with a view to repentance. Righteous judgement begins with honesty before God as each of us examines our life. When we cultivate this self-examination, we destroy the roots of hypocrisy.

- Pray for a heart that is generous in its judgements.

- Pray for forgiveness for those inappropriate and harsh judgements made of others.

- Remember that God loves you and forgives you.

SUNDAY NEXT
BEFORE LENT

MATTHEW 6.16–21

'And whenever you fast, do not look dismal, like the hypocrites, for they disfigure their faces so as to show others that they are fasting. Truly I tell you, they have received their reward.

'But when you fast, put oil on your head and wash your face, so that your fasting may be seen not by others but by your Father who is in secret; and your Father who sees in secret will reward you.

'Do not store up for yourselves treasures on earth, where moth and rust consume and where thieves break in and steal; but store up for yourselves treasures in heaven, where neither moth nor rust consumes and where thieves do not break in and steal.

'For where your treasure is, there your heart will be also.'

COMMENTARY

In the central section of the Sermon on the Mount, we have Jesus' teaching on what Judaism saw as the three religious duties put before faithful people: almsgiving, prayer and fasting. Whatever has been true in the past, there is little doubt that fasting has become the Cinderella. We may give to good causes and say our prayers, but few of us seriously give up food and drink as a religious discipline. However, Lent is still an exception for many Christians (though not often to the level of Ramadan for Muslims). But for all three of our duties, Jesus has important advice: we must keep our eye always on their sole purpose – to deepen our devotion to God. We are not to fast with a view to people thinking how devout we are (still less just to lose weight!). Nor should we make it a time of misery. No, it is for God's sake alone, a self-denying based on love for God.

REFLECTION

In truth, all of our motivations are inclined to be mixed. Any community depends upon a whole number of invisible tasks being done without acknowledgement or reward. However, we sometimes crave recognition, even though we know it is not part of the deal!

So we should look at our motivation. It is a choice we all have to make. Are we doing our good work so that the results of our work will be seen and appreciated by others, or are we doing it because God has called us to do that work? Is our work a job to be done, or is it a prayer to be prayed?

Moreover, in our need for engagement with God, we should see that it will be satisfied when God is sought in candour and simplicity. This Gospel text asks us again to be more interested in where our heart is: is it bound up with a search for security, vulnerable to various forms of decay, or is it engaged in the pursuit of God's will?

- Thank God for the opportunities given to us all to serve him and build up our community.

- Reflect upon your motivation for doing good.

- Give thanks for all those whose invisible work makes our community work so creatively.

ASH WEDNESDAY WEEK

MATTHEW 4.1–11

Then Jesus was led up by the Spirit into the wilderness to be tempted by the devil. He fasted for forty days and forty nights, and afterwards he was famished. The tempter came and said to him, 'If you are the Son of God, command these stones to become loaves of bread.'

But he answered, 'It is written, "One does not live by bread alone, but by every word that comes from the mouth of God."'

Then the devil took him to the holy city and placed him on the pinnacle of the temple, saying to him, 'If you are the Son of God, throw yourself down; for it is written, "He will command his angels concerning you." and "On their hands they will bear you up, so that you will not dash your foot against a stone."'

Jesus said to him, 'Again it is written, "Do not put the Lord your God to the test."'

Again, the devil took him to a very high mountain and showed him all the kingdoms of the world and their splendour; and he said to him, 'All these I will give you, if you will fall down and worship me.'

Jesus said to him, 'Away with you, Satan! for it is written, "Worship the Lord your God, and serve only him."' Then the devil left him, and suddenly angels came and waited on him.

COMMENTARY

The story of Jesus' temptations in the wilderness is always associated with Lent. The season began as the time of final preparation for Easter, especially for those training for baptism on the great day of new life. Then it settled into being a regular time of fasting and discipline for all Christians each year. We should note that the word 'temptation' does not quite get the sense of what is in mind: Jesus underwent three 'tests' of his resolve to serve God's purpose. All three are modelled on tests that came to the people of Israel in their 40-year wanderings in the wilderness after leaving Egypt and on the way to their Promised Land.

Jesus endures and wins through with his fidelity to God intact. With such seriousness of purpose may we approach our lesser testing through Lent.

REFLECTION

Flesh is what we live in – it is how we learn and how we communicate. It is the primary way in which we are connected to each other. Our apprehension of beauty is to do with flesh, and the connecting sense of gift.

To be a friend of God is to learn to be a friend of my own frailty, accepting and affirming it, entrusting it to God. It is recognizing that the self God deals with is not some mysterious inner core, but my body. I am that body, whether young or old, fit or diseased. Who I am is to be seen and known in my own flesh. Bodies are where we learn and where we speak and share. If we can't love our mortal vulnerability, our own frail flesh, we shall be nothing and nobody.

All this is made real in Christ. We are given an opportunity in Lent to attend to our human lives. Broken on the altar, shared for us and, through us, for the world. So we ask our incarnate God to give us the gift of incarnation, the heart of flesh; so to keep us in touch with our mortality and our own special pains that we are free for welcome and compassion, friends with our own vulnerability and so friends with the vulnerable.

- Give thanks to God for your own flesh, your own physicality.
- Pray that God will help you befriend your human limitations.
- Treasure and nurture your vulnerability.

LENT 1

MARK 10.35–45

James and John, the sons of Zebedee, came forward to Jesus and said to him, 'Teacher, we want you to do for us whatever we ask of you.' And he said to them, 'What is it you want me to do for you?' And they said to him, 'Grant us to sit, one at your right hand and one at your left, in your glory.'

But Jesus said to them, 'You do not know what you are asking. Are you able to drink the cup that I drink, or be baptized with the baptism that I am baptized with?'

They replied, 'We are able.' Then Jesus said to them, 'The cup that I drink you will drink; and with the baptism with which I am baptized, you will be baptized; but to sit at my right hand or at my left is not mine to grant, but it is for those for whom it has been prepared.'

When the ten heard this, they began to be angry with James and John. So Jesus called them and said to them, 'You know that among the Gentiles those whom they recognize as their rulers lord it over them, and their great ones are tyrants over them. But it is not so among you; but whoever wishes to become great among you must be your servant, and whoever wishes to be first among you must be slave of all. For the Son of Man came not to be served but to serve, and to give his life a ransom for many.'

COMMENTARY

The subject is the nature of power among the followers of Jesus. Along with that on wealth, no part of Jesus' teaching has proved more intolerable down the centuries. For how can any human society avoid the exercise of power – and with it the temptations to abuse power and for its holders to be corrupted by self-importance and delusions of grandeur – if not worse? In the Gospel of Mark, especially, there is no attempt to show the disciples as 'saints'. On the contrary, they are flawed men – followers of Jesus but failures at every challenge. Jesus puts 'service' as the alternative to 'power' – and himself as dedicated to this cause – to the point of his own death. To be a 'servant' on this scale is a new doctrine indeed.

REFLECTION

Much of the time we are like James and John. We worry about money and power and control. Why are we like this? Why do we pursue positions of power when there is so much more reward in reaching out to others? Perhaps you have heard the beautiful children's story, 'The Tale of Three Trees'. In the story one tree wants to be a cradle, one a mighty ship, and one wants to be simply a tall tree pointing people to God. But then one day the woodcutters come and chop down the three trees and destroy their dreams. The first tree is not made into a cradle, but into a simple feeding trough, a manger for animals. But the manger is sold to a family in Bethlehem and on the night that Jesus is born, that simple feed box becomes the cradle for the Christ child.

The second tree is used to build a boat, but not the kind it had dreamed of – not a mighty ocean-going vessel, but a tiny inexpensive fishing boat. A man named Simon Peter buys the boat and on a warm afternoon when the crowds press in, Jesus himself climbs aboard this small fishing boat so that he might preach good news to the people.

The third tree is also deprived of its dream. It wants to remain standing tall and pointing towards God. Instead, it is cut down and shaped into a horrible instrument of torture, a cross. But it is on this very cross that Jesus is crucified, transforming a symbol of cruelty into a powerful reminder of God's eternal love for all people. The three trees are humbled, but in the plan of God they are exalted.

So that's the way it works. Often our dreams are shattered in life. When our dreams are shattered, we can choose despair and keep hankering after control and power, or we have another choice: we can choose in humility to give ourselves to God. When we make this choice of conversion, we give ourselves to following Jesus in the power of the Cross. When we do this, our Lord can do great acts of service through us – greater than we can ever imagine.

- Pray for all those who exercise power.
- Pray for all those who serve the Church in so many different ways.
- Pray for the gift of humility.

LENT 2

MARK 10.32–34

They were on the road, going up to Jerusalem, and Jesus was walking ahead of them: they were amazed, and those who followed were afraid.

He took the twelve aside again and began to tell them what was to happen to him, saying, 'See, we are going up to Jerusalem, and the Son of Man will be handed over to the chief priests and the scribes, and they will condemn him to death; then they will hand him over to the Gentiles; they will mock him, and spit upon him, and flog him, and kill him; and after three days he will rise again'.

COMMENTARY

Here we read the third and last of three predictions of Jesus' coming Passion to be found in the Gospel of Mark (and repeated in Matthew and Luke). They all come in the latter part of the Gospel, in chapters 8, 9 and 10. They are more than mere predictions. They are statements of Jesus' avowed purpose. He goes to Jerusalem deliberately, knowing what lies in store. This is not an absurd act of sick self-harming. He embraces his future because he believes it to be his God-given role. So Jesus is a willing martyr, that at least. But more than that, he sees his suffering and death as in line with Old Testament passages (like Psalm 22 and Isaiah 53) which view self-offering as opening the door to the good of others.

REFLECTION

I wonder what the word 'Jerusalem' means to you? It comes in many hymns, and we are especially fond of Blake's 'Jerusalem'. Jerusalem is a place of fruition and pilgrimage but also a place of conflict and division.

Jerusalem, as Christians perceive it, is nevertheless first of all a city, or a society, of this world. Then it is a vision that may be built with the bricks of this world, yet in part will always lie beyond this world:

> Blessed city, heavenly Salem,
> Vision dear of peace and love,
> Who of living stones up-builded
> Art the joy of heaven above.

Jerusalem is in part vision and hope. So what we should hope for this Lent is what kind of Jerusalem we want to see, and who it is that might best work together to bring about the kind of society where all flourish. So let us accept the invitation of Jesus to his disciples – that is to say, to you and me – to travel afresh to Jerusalem in these next days which lie between now and Easter.

It will mean each one of us thinking about how we can make our journey to Jerusalem with Jesus and his disciples. We are now going up to Jerusalem. And there you will suffer many things of the powers that be, in Church as well as state. But Jerusalem in this world is not the end of our hopes.

- Thank God for the self-offering of Christ.
- What kind of new Jerusalem might we build together on earth?
- Travel with Jesus towards Jerusalem this Lent.

LENT 3

MARK 10.46–52

*As Jesus and his disciples and a large crowd were leaving Jericho,
Bartimaeus son of Timaeus, a blind beggar, was sitting by the roadside.
When he heard that it was Jesus of Nazareth, he began to shout out
and say, 'Jesus, Son of David, have mercy on me!'*

*Many sternly ordered him to be quiet, but he cried out even more
loudly, 'Son of David, have mercy on me!' Jesus stood still and said, 'Call
him here.' And they called the blind man, saying to him, 'Take heart; get
up, he is calling you.'*

*So throwing off his cloak, he sprang up and came to Jesus. Then Jesus
said to him, 'What do you want me to do for you?' The blind man said
to him, 'My teacher, let me see again.'*

*Jesus said to him, 'Go; your faith has made you well.' Immediately he
regained his sight and followed him on the way.*

COMMENTARY

On the surface, this is simply a story of Jesus healing a blind man. But
for us, as surely for those who first heard it read to them, the story has
deeper and wider meanings. Our physical eyes may function reasonably
well, but there are other kinds of 'blindness' – to our own inner needs,
to the needs of others, to God himself. So Bartimaeus sits, off the road
(itself a metaphor for the way of Jesus). He is both unseeing and in
need – which he recognizes as Jesus comes nearer. Jesus meets his need:
he 'sees' and he 'follows'. He comes to faith and is on the road which
Jesus walks, leading to the Cross. We may do the same.

REFLECTION

Physical sight is not required for discipleship, but restoration is. Again
and again in history, prophecy and gospel, God works through miracles,
through political forces, through social action and through ordinary
living to pick us up from where we have fallen and redirect us along

right pathways. Blind Bartimaeus calls from the gutter until the Lord hears him. Then he returns to the Lord and is restored.

Those who return to the Lord *are* restored, the Bible instructs. This process of restoration may be described in many ways. As we look back, there have been many reformations in the past, but we ourselves and our community should not be blind to the present need for reformation and restoration. This is true not only of the sixteenth century but also of the twenty-first century. Despite Martin Luther King's vision and dream of a just society, there is much to be done about racism and poverty. There are rhythms of reformation. The troublemakers become heroes. The radical new ways eventually become beloved traditions. We are always moving from blindness to sightedness, from unfaithfulness to faithfulness. Reformations teach us that we need to continue to see more clearly, and to reform.

What corners of the Church and of society need serious reformation in this twenty-first century? Where are our blind spots? Will a reformer arise among us? And if one should arise, what would we do to him or her? We disciples of Jesus have vision problems. We sometimes describe our blindness as an inability to see the forest for the tree. More worrisome is the error of blindness of each generation, which so often assumes that it is the best generation of all, with no lessons left to learn, only an inheritance to enjoy. This arrogance is the root of our blindness. We still need the miracle of restored sight.

- Pray for those who work among the visually impaired.
- Ask for God's healing on your own areas of blindness.
- Pray for reformation and change so that we might be faithful to the gospel.

LENT 4

MARK 14.1–9

It was two days before the Passover and the festival of Unleavened Bread. The chief priests and the scribes were looking for a way to arrest Jesus by stealth and kill him; for they said, 'Not during the festival, or there may be a riot among the people.'

While he was at Bethany in the house of Simon the leper, as he sat at the table, a woman came with an alabaster jar of very costly ointment of nard, and she broke open the jar and poured the ointment on his head.

But some were there who said to one another in anger, 'Why was the ointment wasted in this way? For this ointment could have been sold for more than three hundred denarii, and the money given to the poor.' And they scolded her.

But Jesus said, 'Let her alone; why do you trouble her? She has performed a good service for me. For you always have the poor with you, and you can show kindness to them whenever you wish; but you will not always have me.

'She has done what she could; she has anointed my body beforehand for its burial. Truly I tell you, wherever the good news is proclaimed in the whole world, what she has done will be told in remembrance of her.'

COMMENTARY

Perhaps especially in its final words, this is one of the most beautiful stories in Mark's Gospel. Jesus interprets the woman's anointing of his head as a kind of burial-in-advance. (We should then perhaps not be surprised when the later visit of three women to the tomb to anoint Jesus' body proved redundant.) It is both an act of devotion and one of prophecy. And such qualities belong fair and square with the preaching of the good news of salvation 'in the whole world'.

REFLECTION

The purpose of the Gospel is to quicken faith. The purpose of the Church is to nurture faith. What is faith? Most people understand faith in terms of belief. But to speak of faith in terms of belief is to render it – and leave it – one-sidedly cerebral, abstract, what Calvin called 'mere notions flitting about in the brain'. We should understand faith, rather, as the response we render our Lord when he puts question after question to us. The sign of faith, therefore, isn't what we say we believe; the sign of faith, rather, is what we do. If we truly believe, then there is much we shall do. Yet behind the many questions our Lord puts to us at different times, on different occasions, there is one question he puts to us all at all times: 'Do you love me? How much do you love me?'

A woman's poured-out perfume and poured-out heart told our Lord how much she loved him. It should have told the onlookers too. It didn't, however, because they claimed to be concerned for the poor. Her deed couldn't tell onlookers how much she loved him, however, in that they lacked such love themselves. And lacking such love themselves, they were unable to recognize it in someone else.

Then how much do I love him? How much more should I love him? And you?

- Give thanks for the generosity of the gospel.

- Pray for an open and generous response to the love of God in Christ.

- Pray for a deeper devotion to the saving self-offering of Christ.

MOTHERING SUNDAY

COLOSSIANS 3.12–17

As God's chosen ones, holy and beloved, clothe yourselves with compassion, kindness, humility, meekness, and patience. Bear with one another and, if anyone has a complaint against another, forgive each other; just as the Lord has forgiven you, so you also must forgive.

Above all, clothe yourselves with love, which binds everything together in perfect harmony. And let the peace of Christ rule in your hearts, to which indeed you were called in the one body. And be thankful.

Let the word of Christ dwell in you richly; teach and admonish one another in all wisdom; and with gratitude in your hearts sing psalms, hymns, and spiritual songs to God. And whatever you do, in word or deed, do everything in the name of the Lord Jesus, giving thanks to God the Father through him.

COMMENTARY

For many Christians, the middle Sunday of Lent is Mothering Sunday – a day to give presents to mothers, to pray for them, and to remember them with gratitude if they have departed this life. More broadly, it is a day to celebrate family life and to thank God for our own families. So we think especially of the role of family as a school for growth in goodness – partly through its everyday spirit and partly through actual teaching. The passage we read sums up the great features of the virtuous life to which we should direct our hearts, always in the setting of the praise of God.

REFLECTION

On this Mothering Sunday we often look towards Mary who must have embraced significant pain and sadness during her life. I once heard a story about an elderly man who came into an anatomy department in a university to enquire about how he could go about donating his body to medical science. The receptionist gave him the appropriate brochure with all the details. He sat down in the foyer and read the literature. Having read it, he came back to the receptionist and said he would like to proceed. The receptionist handed the man the appropriate forms. He sat down and completed them, returned them to the desk and handed them over. 'Thank you very much,' said the receptionist to the man. 'Where do I go now?' the man asked. Perhaps that man felt so isolated that to him his body was nothing more than an encumbrance from which he longed to be free. Perhaps his life was so bleak and so far spent that to him it was nothing more than a body in need of disposal.

Mary and the beloved disciple at the foot of the Cross set out the true nature of parting and death. Our Lord's laying down of his life, a life in all its fullness, a body of relationships and emotions, attachments and commitments – all these Jesus gives to the life of the world. These Jesus has to let go – in love and faithfulness.

These are realities for us. When should a parent let go and let be? When should a child stop expecting parents to make it all better for them? How can we care and not care? What distance in relationships helps the other to grow, to be free and experience space? Being a mother isn't easy – to be mothered is sometimes hard.

All these things our Lord keeps and mends and completes and perfects. In Christ we may embrace the going in hope and joy: we are always one in him. It is this love that binds us together and finds its beautiful reflection in motherhood. May we put away all that alienates us from God and our fellow human beings by allowing the life of Christ to blossom in us, as we journey on.

- Give thanks today for all women and mothers.
- Pray for families.
- Give thanks for the example of Mary.

LENT 5

ISAIAH 53.3–7

He was despised and rejected by others; a man of suffering and acquainted with infirmity; and as one from whom others hide their faces he was despised, and we held him of no account.

Surely he has borne our infirmities and carried our diseases; yet we accounted him stricken, struck down by God, and afflicted.

But he was wounded for our transgressions, crushed for our iniquities; upon him was the punishment that made us whole, and by his bruises we are healed.

All we like sheep have gone astray; we have all turned to our own way, and the Lord has laid on him the iniquity of us all.

He was oppressed, and he was afflicted, yet he did not open his mouth; like a lamb that is led to the slaughter, and like a sheep that before its shearer is silent, so he did not open his mouth.

COMMENTARY

What better reading can we hear as Holy Week and the Passion of Jesus approaches? It was written some centuries before and its original reference is still uncertain: is it about the suffering of the people of Israel, personified as the servant of God, or is it about an individual, a prophet perhaps who is rejected by those around? Christians were not slow to see it as looking to Jesus and helping us to interpret his suffering and death. It was, after all, not easy at first to see that it had any positive meaning – it was simply, so it seemed, a brutal martyrdom. But we are to look more deeply. The suffering of such a one is 'for us' and mysteriously sets us free. It forces a crisis and we are renewed for God.

REFLECTION

The words of Isaiah describing God's chosen servant offer us a compelling image. As we read this description of God's servant, perhaps

46

we see the face of innocent victims. The faces of the Jews led to death in Auschwitz. Or the face of Damilola Taylor, a young black boy stabbed to death on a south London estate. And many others who have been innocent victims of a world where violence and cruelty are a daily part of life.

There are many other images of human suffering, of horror and of huge injustice. Perhaps we are so familiar with them that our sensitivities are numbed. Vivid images of pain and death and lostness.

What do you see? How do you see? What images fill your hearts and minds? What disturbs and saddens you? How do we engender an authentic encounter and engagement with our world as it is, in all its complexity and pain?

In our own ways, by our attitudes, our actions or our apathy, we have all contributed to each of the awful scenarios because of our share in human sin. These individuals are not victims of a vindictive God, but of our own common failing. Part of growing up spiritually involves accepting our responsibility in and for sin.

When we ponder the awesome mystery of the physical and spiritual realities of the Cross, perhaps we are aware of the dangers of detachment and distance, turning Good Friday more into a picnic than a penance. If, as we begin Holy Week, we are to participate in the events that made this day in history, we must take our place in events that make this day a reality, here and now, for far too many people. Perhaps we should consider where we stand as our Lord is crucified again and again. It is truly heartbreaking. And that's how it should be.

- Pray for all innocent victims of suffering and violence.

- When you reflect on innocence, who do you picture in your mind's eye?

- Spend some time to prepare for your journey through Holy Week towards Easter.

PALM SUNDAY (LENT 6)

MARK 11.1–11

When Jesus and his disciples were approaching Jerusalem, at Bethphage and Bethany, near the Mount of Olives, [Jesus] sent two of his disciples and said to them, 'Go into the village ahead of you, and immediately as you enter it, you will find tied there a colt that has never been ridden; untie it and bring it. If anyone says to you, "Why are you doing this?" just say this, "The Lord needs it and will send it back here immediately."'

They went away and found a colt tied near a door, outside in the street. As they were untying it, some of the bystanders said to them, 'What are you doing, untying the colt?' They told them what Jesus had said; and they allowed them to take it.

Then they brought the colt to Jesus and threw their cloaks on it; and he sat on it. Many people spread their cloaks on the road, and others spread leafy branches that they had cut in the fields.

Then those who went ahead and those who followed were shouting, 'Hosanna! Blessed is the one who comes in the name of the Lord! Blessed is the coming kingdom of our ancestor David! Hosanna in the highest heaven!' Then he entered Jerusalem and went into the temple; and when he had looked around at everything, as it was already late, he went out to Bethany with the twelve.

COMMENTARY

Hearers and readers of the Palm Sunday story should recall the passage in the book of Zechariah (9.9) which is the model for Jesus' action, and shows us its meaning. It is the most kingly and messianic act of Jesus' whole ministry. So it states plainly – for those with eyes to see – an important part of the truth of the Passion. Jesus is first acclaimed and then rejected by those to whom he came as God's anointed agent for their deepest good. There is in Jesus' mission both a local, Jewish aspect, here played out, and a universal aspect – where we come into the picture, belonging to a quite different time and place. Yet we can try to enter, in imagination and devotion, into the raw beginnings of that from which we so richly profit.

REFLECTION

What are the marks of our Christian journey as we follow Christ through this Holy Week? Perhaps they are following, changing and sharing.

First we follow. We follow and journey with Christ through moments of joy and new beginnings, as well as through moments of sorrow and death. From a manger in Bethlehem, the wilderness of temptation through Gethsemane to Calvary. In our own journeys we run the gamut of changing emotions – and at times it must seem difficult to keep faith when we cannot see where we are going. A journey of faith can lead us blindly into the unknown but it is a journey that is shared by the assurance of God's presence.

We follow, and then we pray to be changed. Are we going to keep these remarkable events of this Holy Week to ourselves? Are we to go home, unchanged and unmoved by all we have seen and heard? How is this story going to change us, heal us, transform us? We are here to tell the story of Christ and to show his love in and through our places of living and work. We are followers of Christ who have been changed by our encounter with God.

Then sharing it has its costs and its risks, and it will certainly bring us into conflict because there can be no real sharing of faith without challenge. We live in a society which is in danger of becoming deaf to the music of God's love in Christ. That music is being drowned out by the seductive tones of materialism and consumerism.

How can we be effective witnesses today? Palm Sunday encourages us to keep rejoicing: 'Blessed is he who comes in the name of the Lord.' There is nothing like praise inhabiting the heart for the song of faith to be shared. Effective Christianity stirs our whole being in praise and service; and worship leading to witness.

- What does it mean for you to follow God?

- Ask for God's blessing on your journey of faith.

- Ask for God's help for you to share your faith with others.

MAUNDY THURSDAY

JOHN 13.1–11

Now before the festival of the Passover, Jesus knew that his hour had come to depart from this world and go to the Father. Having loved his own who were in the world, he loved them to the end. The devil had already put it into the heart of Judas son of Simon Iscariot to betray him.

And during supper Jesus, knowing that the Father had given all things into his hands, and that he had come from God and was going to God, got up from the table, took off his outer robe, and tied a towel around himself. Then he poured water into a basin and began to wash the disciples' feet and to wipe them with the towel that was tied around him.

He came to Simon Peter, who said to him, 'Lord, are you going to wash my feet?' Jesus answered, 'You do not know now what I am doing, but later you will understand.'

Peter said to him, 'You will never wash my feet.' Jesus answered, 'Unless I wash you, you have no share with me.' Simon Peter said to him, 'Lord, not my feet only but also my hands and my head!'

Jesus said to him, 'One who has bathed does not need to wash, except for the feet, but is entirely clean. And you are clean, though not all of you.' For he knew who was to betray him; for this reason he said, 'Not all of you are clean.'

COMMENTARY

In the Gospel of John, there are features of the Passion story which are not found in the other Gospels. Most strikingly, while John does not recount the details of the Last Supper itself, he does give this memorable account of Jesus washing the disciples' feet. And he follows it with teaching that helps to give its meaning: 'A new commandment I give to you: that you love one another' (13.35).

('Commandment': in Latin *Mandatum*, in Old English 'Maundy', hence the name for this day in Holy Week.) Peter's objection helps us to see that all of us stand in need of this 'washing'; and the end of pride is essential for us to give ourselves in true and effective devotion to

Jesus – who is God's 'Word' to us, the giver of all light and life and truth. The single action is a gesture summing up the essence of Christian life.

REFLECTION

A young Galilean sat down with his friends and did something very simple, and said something very unusual – intending that in the future his friends should remember. Two acts are at the centre of all that we are – we should recall them for they define our identity. He took bread and broke it, and then he got up from the table and removed his outer garments and washed his friends' feet. The service of love's humility. This is creative leadership – being in the presence of another in all one's weakness. As friends of Jesus we have no power, save the enabling power of love offered. This is the core of our identity; the meaning of Christian discipleship, the purpose of our community. We lay down our security, our reputations, our lives if need be, so that others might live more fully. Love's humility: that we love our Lord in his own people. This worked out in action means that we stand close to God when we listen to others in order to serve. We try to understand each other's needs and aspirations, fears and hopes, whatever they are.

The law of love demands that we become the people of love's humility. Like Christ, we are to wash the feet of our neighbour, no matter how crippled, how dirty – for all those feet have walked within the love of God.

With Jesus, let us put love in where love is not. Through the grace of love's humility, let us continue his example as we kneel girded with the towel of compassion, the watering tears of vulnerability, and with our hearts the basin of acceptance. Jesus has given us the example that we might become love's humility.

- Pray for a deeper devotion to our Lord in the celebration of the Eucharist.
- Pray for the gift of humility and service.
- Resolve yourself to small acts of love.

GOOD FRIDAY

LUKE 23.32–46

Two others also, who were criminals, were led away to be put to death with him. When they came to the place that is called The Skull, they crucified Jesus there with the criminals, one on his right and one on his left. Then Jesus said, 'Father, forgive them; for they do not know what they are doing.'

And they cast lots to divide his clothing. And the people stood by, watching; but the leaders scoffed at him, saying, 'He saved others; let him save himself if he is the Messiah of God, his chosen one!'

The soldiers also mocked him, coming up and offering him sour wine, and saying, 'If you are the King of the Jews, save yourself!' There was also an inscription over him, 'This is the King of the Jews.'

One of the criminals who were hanged there kept deriding him and saying, 'Are you not the Messiah? Save yourself and us!' But the other rebuked him, saying, 'Do you not fear God, since you are under the same sentence of condemnation? And we indeed have been condemned justly, for we are getting what we deserve for our deeds, but this man has done nothing wrong.' Then he said, 'Jesus, remember me when you come into your kingdom.' He replied, 'Truly I tell you, today you will be with me in Paradise.'

It was now about noon, and darkness came over the whole land until three in the afternoon, while the sun's light failed; and the curtain of the temple was torn in two. Then Jesus, crying with a loud voice, said, 'Father, into your hands I commend my spirit.' Having said this, he breathed his last.

COMMENTARY

Each of the narratives of the death of Jesus in the four Gospels has its own way of seeing it, its own angle on its meaning. We consider the special features of Luke's telling of the story. It shows us Jesus dying as he lived, all of a piece. So, first, he prays for his tormentors, even as they crucify him and mock him, just as he has offered divine forgiveness to sinners throughout his ministry. Then there is Jesus' dealing with the criminals crucified alongside him. One sees nothing of the truth and virtue of Jesus; the other turns to him for the remedy he needs. Such 'turning', here as always, meets its immediate reward. Finally, Jesus himself dies, and on his lips are the devout words of surrender to the Father, from Psalm 31.5 – a model for us all.

REFLECTION

It is a popular lie that there can be love without pain and love without sacrifice, that the word 'passion' signifies the pursuit of pleasure only. Such passion is fantasy, and will, in the end, die. True love is love which suffers – and we find this in the love of God, shown in Christ.

We do not know the harm that we do to ourselves and others; sometimes because our motives, which seemed honest beforehand, turn out on reflection to be corrupt.

Part of what we learn from the death of Christ is the central reality of sin and the necessity for us to learn to forgive others. The death of Christ asks us to consider the ways in which we hurt each other. Our life's hurts lie deep within us, fuelling our anger, our fear, our hatred and our scorn, all of which divide us from God and from one another.

Jesus placed forgiveness at the centre of his life and death. Each of us must accept our responsibility for the harm that we do. To admit our guilt is an inevitable part of the hard road to freedom. The outcome is forgiveness. Jesus came to save our disordered race, by calling a halt to anger, revenge and cruelty. In the final moments of terror as the nails are driven through the ankles and wrists there is forgiveness – while bestial humankind, with all the scars of all the ages, is absorbed into the love of God. In this embrace there is healing, forgiveness and transformation.

- Give thanks for all that God has done for us in Christ.

- Pray for forgiveness.

- Pray for an individual or situation where you are finding it difficult to forgive.

EASTER

MARK 16.1–8

When the sabbath was over, Mary Magdalene, and Mary the mother of James, and Salome bought spices, so that they might go and anoint him. And very early on the first day of the week, when the sun had risen, they went to the tomb.

They had been saying to one another, 'Who will roll away the stone for us from the entrance to the tomb?'

When they looked up, they saw that the stone, which was very large, had already been rolled back. As they entered the tomb, they saw a young man, dressed in a white robe, sitting on the right side; and they were alarmed.

But he said to them, 'Do not be alarmed; you are looking for Jesus of Nazareth, who was crucified. He has been raised; he is not here. Look, there is the place they laid him.

'But go, tell his disciples and Peter that he is going ahead of you to Galilee; there you will see him, just as he told you.' So they went out and fled from the tomb, for terror and amazement had seized them; and they said nothing to anyone, for they were afraid.

COMMENTARY

With these words Mark, writer of the oldest Gospel, finishes his book. It is the plainest and most mysterious of all the accounts. It leaves us with questions that hang in the air. Did the meeting of Jesus with his disciples happen? Who is the shadowy 'young man'? If the women 'said nothing to anyone', how did the news ever get out? Other Gospels seek to answer these questions. Mark chose to leave them dangling, creating an air of mystery. Perhaps the truth is that he teaches us a lesson in faith. We are to accept Jesus as our way to God, entering into the gift with trust and love. To have a watertight basis for our relationship with God through Jesus would be to empty it of its necessary character. It is an unfolding quest into love.

REFLECTION

The event of Easter was born precisely because it was an unexpected and life-changing experience for those first disciples. There is always a mystery, a diversity, a greater depth, new things to uncover about the transformation possible because of Easter.

If we delve beneath the surface of these Easter encounters which the Gospels describe, we do not find human strength and resolve. Instead we find fragility: people who are at their lowest point, whose whole world has collapsed. In the case of the disciples, it is because they believed Jesus to have disappeared for ever. In the case of ourselves it may be that we come to Easter with pressing questions that we want to put to God. It is vital that we bring these questions and not try to hide behind them in the beauty and dignity of our Easter celebrations.

Amidst our unanswered questions, part of the Easter truth is to affirm that God is there with us. We need, surely, to take the whole of Jesus' story, the great narrative of life and death, encounter and betrayal, teaching and miracle, and let it speak to us, engage with us, challenge us, and perhaps even shake us up and heal us.

The two foundations of Easter faith are always fragility and love. The difference between God and everyone is that he does not manipulate us into submission through our vulnerability with fancy sales talk. Instead, he gives us the freedom to accept and live our risen life of encounter, renewal and forgiveness.

Easter has made a mark on human history that is indelible, for the Christ who encounters us in all our fragility and in our love is with us Easter morning and every day.

- Open your heart to the life-changing truth of Christ's life.

- Offer to God your experiences of despair.

- Pray for renewal.

EASTER (ALTERNATIVE)

JOHN 20.11-18

But Mary stood weeping outside the tomb. As she wept, she bent over to look into the tomb; and she saw two angels in white, sitting where the body of Jesus had been lying, one at the head and the other at the feet.

They said to her, 'Woman, why are you weeping?' She said to them, 'They have taken away my Lord, and I do not know where they have laid him.'

When she had said this, she turned round and saw Jesus standing there, but she did not know that it was Jesus. Jesus said to her, 'Woman, why are you weeping? For whom are you looking?'

Supposing him to be the gardener, she said to him, 'Sir, if you have carried him away, tell me where you have laid him, and I will take him away.' Jesus said to her, 'Mary!' She turned and said to him in Hebrew, 'Rabbouni!' (which means Teacher).

Jesus said to her, 'Do not hold on to me, because I have not yet ascended to the Father. But go to my brothers and say to them, "I am ascending to my Father and your Father, to my God and your God".' Mary Magdalene went and announced to the disciples, 'I have seen the Lord'; and she told them that he had said these things to her.

COMMENTARY

John's Gospel gives us a number of stories of appearances of Jesus, risen from the dead, to his followers. The first is to Mary Magdalene. As in some other Easter stories, there is an element of mystery about the risen Jesus: he is not immediately recognizable, yet there is no mistaking him and their relationship is wholly secure. These are all borderland encounters, hints of what is both already ours and yet still beyond our grasp. That is how it must be in our relationship with God: both secure and elusive; both dependable yet never fixed in terms of our making. God always has more in store for us – if only we can be ready and open for him.

REFLECTION

Human life is very beautiful; it is also fragile, frail and finite. The Resurrection sets our life's experience within the perspective of God's purpose for our lives, from beginning to end, and his great purposes for the whole of being and time: his acts of creation, redemption and salvation. In this greater perspective, Christ who is risen becomes the touchstone for meaning: he is the light in our darkness, the hope in despair, the triumph in tragedy. In the Resurrection we see that the truth of God in Jesus Christ has entered into the deepest darkness, bringing new light and life. He is the one who gives hope for ourselves and for our world. This is the God who leads us into light.

We live lives utterly immersed in the increasing driven-ness and activity of the 'now'. Today, the Resurrection of Jesus Christ bids us raise our hearts and our eyes to that altogether larger and fuller vision and all that it encompasses – our joys as well as our pains and struggles. In the Resurrection these different experiences of life find their place in the light of humanity.

Easter calls us to see with new eyes – to look in the light of God's loving and eternal purposes for us and his entire creation. We need to be attentive to those deeper spiritual values which let Christ's eternal life flourish in the here and now among us – not just in the Church, but in the neighbourhoods and communities where we live. We need to seek out those areas where God is replenishing our own aliveness, and where God is replenishing the abundant aliveness of others too.

- Treasure the fragility of life and love.
- Give thanks for the life that Christ brings.
- Pray for new eyes to see God.

EASTER 2

JOHN 20.19–29

When it was evening on that day, the first day of the week, and the doors of the house where the disciples had met were locked for fear of the Jews, Jesus came and stood among them and said, 'Peace be with you.'

After he said this, he showed them his hands and his side. Then the disciples rejoiced when they saw the Lord. Jesus said to them again, 'Peace be with you. As the Father has sent me, so I send you.'

When he had said this, he breathed on them and said to them, 'Receive the Holy Spirit. If you forgive the sins of any, they are forgiven them; if you retain the sins of any, they are retained.' But Thomas (who was called the Twin), one of the twelve, was not with them when Jesus came. So the other disciples told him, 'We have seen the Lord.' But he said to them, 'Unless I see the mark of the nails in his hands, and put my finger in the mark of the nails and my hand in his side, I will not believe.'

A week later his disciples were again in the house, and Thomas was with them. Although the doors were shut, Jesus came and stood among them and said, 'Peace be with you.' Then he said to Thomas, 'Put your finger here and see my hands. Reach out your hand and put it in my side. Do not doubt but believe.' Thomas answered him, 'My Lord and my God!'

Jesus said to him, 'Have you believed because you have seen me? Blessed are those who have not seen and yet have come to believe.'

COMMENTARY

Modern sceptics, or rather half-believers, have taken encouragement from the case of 'doubting Thomas' – though the story was hardly written with present-day British culture in mind! All the same, the final giving of blessing to those who come to Christian faith without having 'seen' is a major encouragement, for it applies to all of us. And there may even be an admonition for those later Christians who claim knock-down experiences of Jesus as the basis for their faith: there is a hint that they may not be barking up the finest tree in the forest. There are, anyway, other features in the passage, notably the commission given to the disciples to be channels of God's forgiveness: as arrangements for the orderly working of the Church developed, this authority came to be channelled through the priesthood and handed on in ordination. But behind this is the beginning of the mission of the Christian community: Christians are 'sent' by Christ, just as he was 'sent' by the Father – without loss of authority or impetus.

REFLECTION

The peace of Christ is not meant to be a nice cosy feeling: it is a prelude to being sent out as a witness. Mission begins in the heart of God. It is God in his infinite and unfathomable love, going out to create the universe in the first place, letting things be with a life of their own. It continues by choosing a people to be his own, the people who come to their focus and climax in Jesus. This love continues to go out as the Church responds to that sending out recorded in the Gospel, and it continues to go out to each person, inviting them to share in God's great work. So the mission of the Church, which is fundamental to its identity, is nothing less than a sharing in the mission of God, the going out of God's love to all humanity. It is about keeping the rumour of God alive in the world. That rumour is kept alive only by witness – authentic and credible witness.

The good news of Easter is that as we struggle with that, through all the ups and downs of human existence, through all the vicissitudes and trials, there is an undeviating love that is with us and for us. It is faithful love, and therefore indestructible, and therefore to be trusted. The rebuffed, the strained, the struggling love of God is to be trusted, as the disciples discovered when, on Easter Day, the one in whom the suffering love of God was disclosed to them was found to be still there, constant and everlasting. To this, through our life and death, we are witnesses.

- Be honest about your doubts and questions, like Thomas.
- Reflect upon the ways that you witness to the gospel of God's love.
- Give thanks for the indestructible and everlasting love of God.

EASTER 3

JOHN 17.6-10

Jesus said, 'I have made your name known to those whom you gave me from the world. They were yours, and you gave them to me, and they have kept your word.

'Now they know that everything you have given me is from you; for the words that you gave to me I have given to them, and they have received them and know in truth that I came from you; and they have believed that you sent me.

'I am asking on their behalf; I am not asking on behalf of the world, but on behalf of those whom you gave me, because they are yours.

'All mine are yours, and yours are mine; and I have been glorified in them.'

COMMENTARY

In many ways, chapter 17 is the climax of the Gospel of John, at least as far as its teaching is concerned. It reads like an intricate piece of verbal tapestry, each sentence taking us a step further in our understanding of God. But it does not stop there: it also serves to draw us into the web of relationship which Jesus expounds. He himself is the centre, bringing us into the relationship with the Father which has been his for ever – 'from the beginning'. God's purpose, brought to pass in and through Jesus, is that we should all be united in his love. The opportunity to seize with both hands is put within our grasp.

REFLECTION

Being an inheritor is something quite a lot of us look forward to and in due course experience. It can be one of life's deeper pleasures – despite the problems that can go with it, from family jealousies to death duties. What is so satisfying about it? Well, there might be simply the pleasure of new wealth, removing anxiety perhaps. But at a deeper level, there is the satisfaction of taking over from someone whom one has loved and maybe revered. Their mantle has come onto your own shoulders. That is the ideal kind of inheritance. It gives you the chance not only to enjoy what you have received but also, if possible, to carry forward what that person stood for. Something like this goes on here in Jesus' 'bequest' of himself to his followers. They now have the awesome responsibility of developing all that he was and stood for. Is it not also a delight?

- Pray for the unity of Christ's Church.

- Ask people to pray for you on your behalf.

- Pray for the vocation of the Church to be distinctive and different.

EASTER 4

JOHN 21.15-19

When they had finished breakfast, Jesus said to Simon Peter, 'Simon son of John, do you love me more than these?' He said to him, 'Yes, Lord; you know that I love you.' Jesus said to him, 'Feed my lambs.'

A second time he said to him, 'Simon son of John, do you love me?' He said to him, 'Yes, Lord; you know that I love you.' Jesus said to him, 'Tend my sheep.'

He said to him the third time, 'Simon son of John, do you love me?' Peter felt hurt because he said to him the third time, 'Do you love me?' And he said to him, 'Lord, you know everything; you know that I love you.' Jesus said to him, 'Feed my sheep. Very truly, I tell you, when you were younger, you used to fasten your own belt and to go wherever you wished. But when you grow old, you will stretch out your hands, and someone else will fasten a belt around you and take you where you do not wish to go.'

(He said this to indicate the kind of death by which he would glorify God.) After this he said to him, 'Follow me.'

COMMENTARY

The apostles chosen by Jesus have always been revered as the first pastors of the Church, shepherds of the Christian flock. Several episodes in the Gospels, this one included, give Peter a central place. Our passage sees 'love' as the required bond between Lord and apostle. To us, this seems to indicate an emotional bond and we may wonder how anyone can demand love from another person. But though that aspect is by no means excluded, loyalty is likely to be more central in the dialogue described. Such loyalty and strength of bond may stretch as far as death in the Lord's cause: and it is clear that Peter suffered this fate, in Rome, some 30 years after the crucifying of his Master in Jerusalem. 'Following' may have the greatest cost.

REFLECTION

It was Bishop John Robinson who said that we are not called to be religious, we are called to be alive. And if we are to be alive, if we are to live out a relationship that is characterized by astonishment at the wonder of what makes us loved and who our lover is, then it is the activity of God, not words about God, that we shall want; and experience of the risen Christ, not an explanation.

We live in a shadow land in which we build our tentative and compromised acts of love for our lover-God upon intangible, subtle and symbolic certainties. God unveils God's self in a light that illumines even as it blinds, in ravishing desire that stirs the senses. That dazzling light that brings darkness is the symbol of what will happen to Paul, the journey of abnegation that he will have to undertake, letting go of his own sight and learning to see with Jesus' eyes.

Peter and Paul, founders of the Church, both accept their responsibility for God's people because they know their own need. Could this be some kind of parable for the Church? Could it be that we are not actually called always to be right, but simply to demonstrate by our own gratitude and love that God can and will forgive? If God can go on loving and forgiving the Church, which has been such a sorry mess for so much of its history, then his power to love and forgive must be enormous indeed.

God has had great love for us. What we have to do is to be grateful and pass it on.

- Thank God for life.
- Pray for transformation.
- Pray for the sharing of God's love.

EASTER 5

LUKE 24.28–32, 35

As they came near the village to which they were going, he walked ahead as if he were going on. But they urged him strongly, saying, 'Stay with us, because it is almost evening and the day is now nearly over.' So he went in to stay with them.

When he was at the table with them, he took bread, blessed and broke it, and gave it to them. Then their eyes were opened, and they recognized Jesus; and he vanished from their sight.

They said to each other, 'Were not our hearts burning within us while he was talking to us on the road, while he was opening the scriptures to us?' . . . Then they told what had happened on the road, and how he had been known to them in the breaking of the bread.

COMMENTARY

The story of the two unnamed followers of Jesus who on Easter Day walk from Jerusalem to the village of Emmaus and are joined by a mysterious companion is one of the most moving in the Gospels. Luke tells it with great artistry and it dominates his final chapter, telling of the first Easter. The two travellers only recognize Jesus when he 'breaks bread' with them. We are to see that the solemn act of the Eucharist is one of Jesus' chief legacies to his people. It is a supreme moment of recognition, when our allegiance to Christ and our enjoyment of his self-giving are at their most intense. The story ends: 'He was known to them in the breaking of the bread.'

REFLECTION

Some of us are better than others at recognizing people when we run into them unexpectedly. Worst of all is when they know who we are while we blunder on 'in the dark'! It can be a road to embarrassment – or even worse. But it can, by contrast, lead to deeper knowledge. Certainly, it is unlikely to happen twice with the same person! So maybe the guiding rule is always to profit from the experience: get the other person fixed in your mind, turn the casual acquaintance into a friend. Then you are learning something about how to attend truly to other people. And in the relationship with people, in Eucharist, in prayer, is a chance to go further and to make more of what we have already received.

- Give thanks for the presence of Jesus accompanying us on our journeys.

- Pray that we may recognize the divine in and through the ordinary.

- Pray that our lives may be challenged by the surprise of God's revelation.

EASTER 6

LUKE 24.44–53

Then Jesus said to the disciples, 'These are my words that I spoke to you while I was still with you – that everything written about me in the law of Moses, the prophets, and the psalms must be fulfilled.'

Then he opened their minds to understand the scriptures, and he said to them, 'Thus it is written, that the Messiah is to suffer and to rise from the dead on the third day, and that repentance and forgiveness of sins is to be proclaimed in his name to all nations, beginning from Jerusalem.

'You are witnesses of these things. And see, I am sending upon you what my Father promised; so stay here in the city until you have been clothed with power from on high.'

Then he led them out as far as Bethany, and, lifting up his hands, he blessed them. While he was blessing them, he withdrew from them and was carried up into heaven.

And they worshipped him, and returned to Jerusalem with great joy; and they were continually in the temple blessing God.

COMMENTARY

The Gospel of Luke finishes with the final hours of Easter Day, after he has told us of the walk to Emmaus. The walkers return to Jerusalem and report their great news to the assembled disciples. Jesus appears in their midst and it is as if he gives to them the essence of his legacy. There are two aspects: first, the bond with the history of Israel as God's people and its leading straight into the coming and death of Jesus, the Messiah. Second, there will be the coming mission in Jesus' name (whose story Luke will tell in the Acts of the Apostles). Here, we are at the join between part one and part two. Jesus withdraws and the disciples will go to the Temple for prayer. Luke's Gospel began there and now it ends there. Continuity with the old is important as well as the great new gift of Christ.

REFLECTION

We can give thanks to God for Luke and the skilled way with which he tells us the story of Christ. In this passage we are reminded of some of the themes that run through his text. We are reminded that our witness to Jesus, to the Gospel and to mission is to all the nations. We need to attend to Scripture carefully to discern God's strategy in inaugurating the reign of justice and peace.

We are witnesses, who are not allowed to put the book down like a good novel and return to business as usual, but are mandated to proclaim the story, to call for repentance, to declare divine forgiveness. We, like the original heroes, are to be recipients of the power that the Father promises, an indication that God intends the plans to be completed and the divine strategy to work.

Finally this narrative ends in an amazing outburst of worship. Their joy and prayer is deep and life-changing. Worship and witness belong together, like the bud that will not bloom without regular watering. The Church's mission dries up without the renewal of worship. This singing of hymns, the prayers of thanksgiving and intercession, the reading and exposition of Scripture, the breaking of bread, keep the Church in touch with the promised power of the Father and make possible the glorifying and enjoying of God in and through the world. Worship becomes the occasion when the story that must be told and re-told among all nations is heard afresh and when the witness to the word is re-envisioned.

- Thank God for Luke's skill in telling the story of Christ.

- Pray for a deeper sense of God's purpose as expressed in Scripture.

- Ask for God's help in the renewal of your vision and the empowering of your witness to him.

ASCENSION

ACTS 1.1–11

In the first book, Theophilus, I wrote about all that Jesus did and taught from the beginning until the day when he was taken up to heaven, after giving instructions through the Holy Spirit to the apostles whom he had chosen.

After his suffering he presented himself alive to them by many convincing proofs, appearing to them over the course of forty days and speaking about the kingdom of God.

While staying with them, he ordered them not to leave Jerusalem, but to wait there for the promise of the Father. 'This', he said, 'is what you have heard from me; for John baptized with water, but you will be baptized with the Holy Spirit not many days from now.'

So when they had come together, they asked him, 'Lord, is this the time when you will restore the kingdom to Israel?' He replied, 'It is not for you to know the times or periods that the Father has set by his own authority. But you will receive power when the Holy Spirit has come upon you; and you will be my witnesses in Jerusalem, in all Judea and Samaria, and to the ends of the earth.'

When he had said this, as they were watching, he was lifted up, and a cloud took him out of their sight. While he was going and they were gazing up towards heaven, suddenly two men in white robes stood by them. They said 'Men of Galilee, why do you stand looking upwards towards heaven? This Jesus, who has been taken up from you into heaven, will come in the same way as you saw him go into heaven.'

COMMENTARY

Luke started his second volume, the Acts of the Apostles, by marking the transition from the lifetime of Jesus, active in the world of his day, to the gradual growth of the Church and its mission, spreading the story of Jesus' teaching, death and Resurrection across the lands of the eastern and northern sides of the Mediterranean. Between the two phases and joining them together comes the episode of Jesus' tangible departure.

It could be a moment of negative feelings – intense emptiness and grief, the signs of bereavement. Instead, it is put before us as a moment of hope – soon to be wholly justified. For us, the message is surely that God is always on the side of the future, with hope and with the endless possibility of good.

REFLECTION

In many Ascension Day hymns and prayers the whole of human nature is spoken of as being raised to heaven in the Ascension. But Jesus is the presence of God's promise in our world, and if the Ascension means that, through the power of the Resurrection, we now share that same calling, then two things follow. First, we as Christian believers are in heaven, but not so as to remove us from this world. In the middle of our life we are given the opportunity to share in God's perspective on things, so that God through us may make his loving faithfulness real and effective here and now. Second, the things and persons of this world are perhaps seen in a new way, charged with glory and hope and promise. They are seen as if already part of the new heaven and new earth in which God's purposes are to be brought to completion.

The Ascension celebrates the new Creation, the bringing together of heaven and earth. When Jesus is seen no more in the old way, that does not mean he has abandoned the world, so that we must go and look for him outside it. His life is being lived in us: the new world is being brought to birth in us, gradually and sometimes painfully. We are caught up in the eternal movement of God's commitment to his creation. In and through Jesus, we too have become a sign of promise. The morning has come and the daystar from on high has dawned upon us.

- Pray for your witness.
- Thank God for earth's glimpses of heaven.
- Pray for God's perspective to shape your life.

EASTER 7

JOHN 15.12–17

Jesus said to his disciples: 'This is my commandment, that you love one another as I have loved you. No one has greater love than this, to lay down one's life for one's friends.

'You are my friends if you do what I command you. I do not call you servants any longer, because the servant does not know what the master is doing; but I have called you friends, because I have made known to you everything that I have heard from my Father.

'You did not choose me but I chose you. And I appointed you to go and bear fruit, fruit that will last, so that the Father will give you whatever you ask him in my name.

'I am giving you these commands so that you may love one another.'

COMMENTARY

As Eastertide draws towards its final period, we reflect on its abiding message for our lives. Almost all the writers to be met in the New Testament give pride of place to the command to love. Often we read of the dual command, drawn in fact from the old Scriptures of Judaism: to love God with all our energies and in all aspects of our being; and to love other people as we care about ourselves. The accent here, in the Gospel of John, is rather different. The followers of Jesus must love 'one another'. The emphasis falls on the bond, intense and close, that must unite Christians – because of their shared relationship with Jesus. As for what it means in detail, that is left to be worked out in our common life.

REFLECTION

While walking in Shropshire I was surprised. Surprised by the horse-chestnut trees. Suddenly in the distance I was captured by their height and depth, their richness and colour – wonderful green expansive leaves and towering blossoms and flowers, whites and pinks. All this beauty set in a field of abundant cow parsley.

Of course I had seen horse chestnuts before, but now they mediated and expressed something profound. They spoke to me of the colour and life, super-abundant life, at the heart of our created order: Earth's immeasurable capacity to surprise if only we look, and see beyond the looking.

In Christ all shall be made alive. God desires for us life; more than physical existence – a depth and purpose, a meaning and direction that can comfort and inspire. God desires for us fullness of life. This is the message of Jesus which, if we will grasp it, will unlock the door and lead us beyond ourselves into life.

The Christian life is always a vocation, hearing the voice of the one who calls us and leads us out – who can and does surprise us. Evocation – calling us out of the relative security of where we are by enabling us to respond to the moment of miracle which is before us. Those who do respond are led into immeasurable surprise. We are born in hills still covered in snow. But Easter bears a promise – the glory which we could not imagine in advance. Life in all its fullness: surprising us by immeasurable depth, opportunity and promise.

- Pray that the Easter message will abide in you.

- Pray for a new vision to see afresh and be surprised by the wonder of creation.

- Pray that through our seeing and surprise we may be changed in love.

PENTECOST/WHITSUNDAY

ACTS 2.1-11

When the day of Pentecost had come, they were all together in one place. And suddenly from heaven there came a sound like the rush of a violent wind, and it filled the entire house where they were sitting. Divided tongues, as of fire, appeared among them, and a tongue rested on each of them. All of them were filled with the Holy Spirit and began to speak in other languages, as the Spirit gave them ability.

Now there were devout Jews from every nation under heaven living in Jerusalem. And at this sound the crowd gathered and was bewildered, because each one heard them speaking in the native language of each. Amazed and astonished, they asked, 'Are not all these who are speaking Galileans? And how is it that we hear, each of us, in our own native language? Parthians, Medes, Elamites, and residents of Mesopotamia, Judea and Cappadocia, Pontus and Asia, Phrygia and Pamphylia, Egypt and the parts of Libya belonging to Cyrene, and visitors from Rome, both Jews and proselytes, Cretans and Arabs – in our own languages we hear them speaking about God's deeds of power.'

COMMENTARY

The story of the first Whitsunday of the Church is sensational indeed. It acts as a kind of trailer for the coming development of the Church and the spread of the message. It is the Jewish feast of Pentecost, one of the days when many made pilgrimage to Jerusalem. They came from all parts of the known world where Jewish colonies had settled. Their languages were many and diverse, but the power of the apostles' preaching overcame the barriers of understanding – it was wonderful and unforgettable. It was a dream not always realized since, but we should still be stirred.

REFLECTION

We divide into haters of what is new and those who can never have enough of it. We are preservers or innovators. You would never guess it, but the Christian faith got going in a burst of novelty: it was the boost that enabled the rocket to surge forth. You would never guess it, because through most of its history and in most of its parts, the Church has set great store by sticking to tradition. Of course, it never quite works – in two ways. However 'traditional' – 'faithful' is the word we like to use – Christians are, they have in fact always adapted, always developed: and so in part deceived themselves! So too with those who in the name of God have gone in for radical novelty – often in the name of restoring the 'true tradition'! They too have soon developed fixed ways of believing and worshipping. The Holy Spirit has a hard time of getting through to us in the interests of our ever-fresh and ever-faithful God!

- Reflect on the way in which the Spirit of God's love is at work in your life.

- Spend some time looking at what you can do in learning to look, to listen and to love.

- Pray for the transformation of God's Spirit.

TRINITY SUNDAY

ISAIAH 6.1–8

In the year that King Uzziah died, I saw the Lord sitting on a throne, high and lofty; and the hem of his robe filled the temple. Seraphs were in attendance above him; each had six wings: with two they covered their faces, and with two they covered their feet, and with two they flew. And one called to another and said:

*'Holy, holy, holy is the L*ORD *of hosts; the whole earth is full of his glory.'*

*The pivots on the thresholds shook at the voices of those who called, and the house filled with smoke. And I said: 'Woe is me! I am lost, for I am a man of unclean lips, and I live among a people of unclean lips: yet my eyes have seen the King, the L*ORD *of hosts!'*

Then one of the seraphs flew to me, holding a live coal that had been taken from the altar with a pair of tongs. The seraph touched my mouth with it and said: 'Now that this has touched your lips, your guilt has departed and your sin is blotted out.'

COMMENTARY

We read this passage from Isaiah around Trinity Sunday because it speaks impressively (even if in an old Jewish way) of the sheer majesty of God. Try as we may, we cannot sum him up: we cannot contain him in any human words – and the more we think we have managed to do it, the more we need to turn aside, think again – and simply worship. Of course the words of a passage like this may easily strike us as strange, but some of them ('Holy, holy, holy . . .') are still at the centre of our worship as we seek to approach the mystery of God and be aware of his holiness and his love.

REFLECTION

There are many things that stimulate our senses. Different kinds of flowers or a particular piece of visual art may give us refreshment. A walk with friends in the countryside may give us a feeling of the grandeur and mystery which is at the heart of the creation and points to its immensity.

In one sense, God is beyond description, beyond human representation and beyond all knowing. We should know the un-knowability of God, who nevertheless both reaches out to us and touches us. Our God has made himself known in the events and activities of the Bible, the blessing of Abraham, the giving of the Promised Land, and in Jesus – active, healing and saving us. God as creator, sustainer, saviour. We ask ourselves how we can conform to him. By sanctification, by becoming like him. In this love and movement which is creative and co-operative, there is a constant flow, a continual and delightful traffic which we call Trinity. The Trinity is the invitation to realize within ourselves the corresponding nature of community, of love, of self-donation which is the image of God in us who are the products of his wonderful creation.

- Give thanks to God for the glimpses of his glory in and through creation.

- Give thanks to God for the challenge of Christ and his gospel.

- Pray for the guidance of God's Spirit in your life.

CORPUS CHRISTI/ THANKSGIVING FOR HOLY COMMUNION

MARK 14.22–25

While they were eating, [Jesus] took a loaf of bread, and after blessing it he broke it, gave it to them, and said, 'Take; this is my body.'

Then he took a cup, and after giving thanks he gave it to them, and all of them drank from it.

He said to them, 'This is my blood of the covenant, which is poured out for many. Truly I tell you, I will never again drink of the fruit of the vine until that day when I drink it new in the kingdom of God.'

COMMENTARY

On the Thursday after Trinity Sunday, many Christians have long expressed devotion to the Holy Sacrament of the Body of Christ. For many, it stands for the regularly received gift of Holy Communion, and it reminds us of its simple beginnings in the closest connection with Jesus' death for us – which it foreshadowed. The devout mystery of the Last Supper, of Calvary and all that has followed, is brought home to us as we worship at this time and seek, however feebly, to return God's love.

REFLECTION

Christianity gives us much to think about and to contemplate, but above all it gives us actions to do. In the Eucharist, what are we doing? In the Eucharist we do the act of sacrifice, of offering. We take everything we are and everything we have. We take everything Christ is and everything Christ did, and we hand it all over to God at the altar as one single offering.

CORPUS CHRISTI/
THANKSGIVING FOR
HOLY COMMUNION

In the Eucharist we also receive. In our lives we need the grace of Communion; it is not an option. We need to feed on Christ, drink his life and love into ourselves. Feed on him in your hearts, bring your need, be poor here, open your hands.

In the Eucharist we are sharing. 'Do this,' we are told, and we are doing together as we were told. Christ at the very table of his betrayal and abandonment gives us the Eucharist, the Holy Communion, so that we can do something to experience the mystery of his love in actuality, the reality that we are all one, all interconnected, all members of a single body, breathing the same breath.

May our celebration and participation in the Eucharist deepen our sense of offering, receiving and sharing.

- Remember before God all those who have been faithful to the command, 'Do this.'

- Spend some time to prepare for your participation in the Eucharist.

- Give thanks for the mystery of this sacrifice given for you.

PROPER 4

MATTHEW 11.25–30

At that time Jesus said, 'I thank you, Father, Lord of heaven and earth, because you have hidden these things from the wise and the intelligent and have revealed them to infants; yes, Father, for such was your gracious will.

'All things have been handed over to me by my Father; and no one knows the Son except the Father, and no one knows the Father except the Son and anyone to whom the Son chooses to reveal him.

'Come to me, all you that are weary and are carrying heavy burdens, and I will give you rest. Take my yoke upon you, and learn from me; for I am gentle and humble in heart, and you will find rest for your souls. For my yoke is easy, and my burden is light.'

COMMENTARY

This passage (also to be found in the Gospel of Luke) reminds us of the great discourses in John 14–17: in its disclosure of the inner relation between the Father and the Son it is unusual in the earlier Gospels, to be compared only to the prayer in Gethsemane before Jesus' arrest. We notice that, as in John, the intimacy of relationship between Father and Son is opened to those whom Jesus chooses. It is divine gift, readily bestowed: that is indeed the point of Jesus' coming. But, in the light of the stringency of Jesus' teaching about the kind of life required of us, we may bridle at his yoke being described as 'easy' and his burden 'light'. The key is that following Jesus is not burdensome because it is done in his company and by his power. So it has the mark of Sabbath joy, active 'rest' for our lives.

REFLECTION

There is something encouragingly spiritual about children and their response to God. We need to learn from their imagination and creativity – the way they share, enjoy and rejoice in things spiritual. If we could only sometimes see as children do, our perception and understanding might be transformed.

I am constantly moved by the wisdom that children express, in ways which are both simple and profound. The honesty of their anger about world poverty, unnecessary war and killing, the futility and fragility of human life in the face of illness and death, reveals a perception of the world which has great integrity and honesty.

Children's preparedness to interrogate and question, to see the gaps and contradictions in an answer; to want to know more about who God is and how God would have us to live – this encourages us towards a spiritual curiosity which could bring us rewards and opportunities for wisdom.

And finally, the simplicity and depth of their prayer in worship is liberated from all of our adult cynicism, materialism and activity. With open hearts they search for the words with which to plead, pray and praise. Children's listening and responding could bring our adult world more delight and wonder at the sheer beauty of God.

- Give thanks for all children and what we learn from them.
- Pray to see and respond as children do.
- In prayer, lay some of your burdens before God.

PROPER 5

LUKE 10.25-37

A lawyer stood up to test Jesus. 'Teacher,' he said, 'what must I do to inherit eternal life?' He said to him, 'What is written in the law? What do you read there?' He answered, 'You shall love the Lord your God with all your heart, and with all your soul, and with all your strength, and with all your mind; and your neighbour as yourself.' And he said to him, 'You have given the right answer; do this, and you will live.'

But wanting to justify himself, he asked Jesus, 'And who is my neighbour?' Jesus replied, 'A man was going down from Jerusalem to Jericho, and fell into the hands of robbers, who stripped him, beat him, and went away, leaving him half dead.

'Now by chance a priest was going down that road; and when he saw him, he passed by on the other side. So likewise a Levite, when he came to the place and saw him, passed by on the other side.

'But a Samaritan while travelling came near him; and when he saw him, he was moved with pity. He went to him and bandaged his wounds, having poured oil and wine on them. Then he put him on his own animal, brought him to an inn, and took care of him.

'The next day he took out two denarii, gave them to the innkeeper, and said, "Take care of him; and when I come back, I will repay you whatever more you spend." Which of these three, do you think, was a neighbour to the man who fell into the hands of the robbers?' He said, 'The one who showed him mercy.' Jesus said to him, 'Go and do likewise.'

COMMENTARY

The parable of the good Samaritan is one of the most familiar parts of the Gospels, and its message seems clear. How do we love our neighbour? Well, by meeting the crying needs of anyone whom we encounter, even those to whom custom gives us no obligations. That is obvious. It is less obvious where the fault of the priest and the Levite lies. It is not that they are callous Jewish clerics who fall at what seems an elementary model hurdle. It is rather that they are virtuous by the requirements of their role: their duties in the temple of Jerusalem meant that they simply must remain in a state of ritual purity – and this would be put at risk by contact with (what might be) a corpse. The idea is so foreign to us now that it is hard to absorb, though it is far from foreign to the other faiths around us – and many Christians have their taboos, people they would 'rather not associate with'. Jesus would have none of it.

REFLECTION

The third traveller, a Samaritan, is the core surprise of this story. He was not simply a good-playing practical man whose generous response exposed the absurdity, even the hypocrisy of the ecclesiastical establishment. To the Samaritan, the Jew who fell among thieves, by long and bitter historical tradition was a sworn enemy. The goodness of the good Samaritan was not, then, simply the natural goodness of the ordinary man who can be relied on to do the decent thing: it was the extraordinary goodness of the man who was ready to regard his worst traditional enemy as his neighbour.

The point of the parable is as sharp as that. Not to be a decent human being, but to help your neighbour and to love your enemy. Even to put it that way is, however, to blunt the point. For the enmity was not personal and, therefore, within the scope of an individual to control and overcome: it was national enmity – deep-seated, emotional and irrational, the product of centuries of Jewish nationalism. It was not then the callousness, even less clericalism, which Jesus in his story of the good Samaritan intended to expose and condemn, but a shallow and cosy, self-satisfied decency. So let us be aware of restricting the meaning of the word 'neighbour'. This parable challenges us to respond – how ready is our generosity to go beyond easy or conventional grounds?

- Who are our enemies and might we try to love them?
- Give thanks for all those who have shown you small acts of kindness.
- How generous are our hearts? Pray that we might become more deeply and radically generous.

PROPER 6

LUKE 10.38-42

Now as Jesus and his disciples went on their way, he entered a certain village, where a woman named Martha welcomed him into her home.

She had a sister named Mary, who sat at the Lord's feet and listened to what he was saying.

But Martha was distracted by her many tasks; so she came to Jesus and asked, 'Lord, do you not care that my sister has left me to do all the work by myself? Tell her then to help me.'

But the Lord answered her, 'Martha, Martha, you are worried and distracted by many things; there is need of only one thing. Mary has chosen the better part, which will not be taken away from her.'

COMMENTARY

This brief story, which easily gives generous-hearted and busily active Christians a discouraging signal, should be valued for its positive message. It puts the accent on the central place of devotion of the heart to Christ in the life of discipleship, and we can let that message stand. For there is no doubt that there is much in all our lives to push simple attention to God, in quiet, unhurried reflection, to the margins. There always seem to be more pressing things to do. At the same time, to go for 'the better part' does not imply there is no value in the rest.

REFLECTION

Too often we have devalued, marginalized and oppressed women within the Christian community. We do well to think about Mary and Martha and the stereotypes with which we imprison women. There are some wonderful features to this story. Think about the warmth and generosity of Martha's welcoming Jesus into her home. Christian hospitality – the conversations and refreshment that we share – deepens community and enlarges our humanity. And for those of us who enjoy others' hospitality, some awareness of the sheer effort and attention that has gone into the sharing of a home and food is surely important.

Second, in all of our families there are rifts and conflicts that express themselves in different ways. Within the Christian family we need to acknowledge the diversity of personalities and gifts, and hold them together even when we have varied perspectives and disagreements.

As it has been often said, we need to be, perhaps, Mary *and* Martha. Doing without listening can easily degenerate into business that loses its purpose. Listening without doing becomes no more than a mockery of the words we have heard. We need both a silent and patient waiting upon God's word and truth and then to build upon our response of decisive activity in building a solid foundation, in maturing in good soil, in being a member of Jesus' family and in being truly blessed. Both Mary and Martha are faithful but in different ways, and we ask that we might imitate them.

- Pray that we may simply attend to God.

- Give thanks for the hospitality of others.

- Help us to live together in and through the richness of our diverse perspectives and personalities.

PROPER 7

LUKE 11.1-8

Jesus was praying in a certain place, and after he had finished, one of his disciples said to him, 'Lord, teach us to pray, as John taught his disciples.'

He said to them, 'When you pray, say: Father, hallowed be your name. Your kingdom come. Give us each day our daily bread. And forgive us our sins, for we ourselves forgive everyone indebted to us. And do not bring us to the time of trial.'

And he said to them, 'Suppose one of you has a friend, and you go to him at midnight and say to him, "Friend, lend me three loaves of bread; for a friend of mine has arrived, and I have nothing to set before him." And he answers from within, "Do not bother me; the door has already been locked, and my children are with me in bed; I cannot get up and give you anything."

'I tell you, even though he will not get up and give him anything because he is his friend, at least because of his persistence he will get up and give him whatever he needs.'

COMMENTARY

Luke's Gospel shows us Jesus as particularly insistent on prayer – and on the need to stick at it. The last part of the passage is to be read with tongue in cheek. We are to go on and on at God who may strike us as being like a grumpy man who does not take to being disturbed in the middle of the night, even by his friends. As to the tone of our prayer, Jesus gives us a model: the keynote is always that God's will may be done. Our whole aim is to align ourselves with God rather than go for our own self-interest.

REFLECTION

Prayer is a central part of the Christian life. In this passage we are reminded that God is addressed as 'Father' and so we disciples are invited to pray with the same familiarity. The fact that the one to whom we pray can be thought of in such an intimate way affects the confidence which we can have in the offering of our prayers. Second, we note that the model prayer is exclusively petitionary. It contains no adoration, thanksgiving or confession, only five requests for God to do something. The disciples are taught what their real needs are and to whom they need to go for satisfaction. God in turn is being asked to fulfil his promises regarding his name, his reign and his care and protection.

We are also reminded of the high value placed on hospitality. God is contrasted with the unfriendly neighbour. If the neighbour who is initially prone to refuse requests finally responds, how much more will God respond to the pleas of the people of God? God can be trusted. Ask, search, knock, for God is not reluctant or hesitant. Prayer is rooted in the kindliness and generosity of God, thus making it possible for us unworthy and stumbling disciples to offer petitions for our life's journey.

- Pray that the Spirit of God may resource you for your Christian discipleship.

- Think about the opportunities God gives to you to offer hospitality to strangers.

- Align yourselves with God and pray regularly.

PROPER 8

LUKE 14.16–24

Then Jesus said to him, 'Someone gave a great dinner and invited many. At the time for the dinner he sent his slave to say to those who had been invited, "Come; for everything is ready now."

'But they all alike began to make excuses. The first said to him, "I have bought a piece of land, and I must go out and see it; please accept my apologies." Another said, "I have bought five yoke of oxen, and I am going to try them out; please accept my apologies." Another said, "I have just been married, and therefore I cannot come."

'So the slave returned and reported this to his master. Then the owner of the house became angry and said to his slave, "Go out at once into the streets and lanes of the town and bring in the poor, the crippled, the blind and the lame." And the slave said, "Sir, what you ordered has been done, and there is still room."

'Then the master said to the slave, "Go out into the roads and lanes, and compel people to come in, so that my house may be filled. For I tell you, none of those who were invited will taste my dinner."'

COMMENTARY

If we try to think what Jesus had in mind when this story was first told, we have to be alive to the situation in his time and place. It began in a Jewish setting when the division between Jews and Gentiles (that is, everybody else!) was deep. Only the Jews would be the heirs of God's promises of perfect peace and prosperity. All others, if they had any place at all, would be second-class citizens. (The picture is not entirely unfamiliar.) What's more, strict Jews believed that even among their own people only those who kept the Law strictly would be rewarded. Jesus, by contrast, proclaims God's open-house policy. It is precisely those who are 'unqualified' who are his chosen ones. In his ministry, Jesus worked out such a vision of things: we 'qualify' most by not deserving to! It was a revolutionary thought.

REFLECTION

You can get a feeling from this story that God is deeply worried about good manners. And perhaps he is when it's a matter of upsetting kind people by our self-centred behaviour. But, as usual with the parables of Jesus, deeper things are at stake. Even if we stay at the superficial level, we can reflect that turning down the willing generosity of others can, in certain circumstances, be gross uncharity, even cruelty.

But the deeper level tells of God's hoped-for relationship with the human race – and with each member of it. What is more, there is always urgency, for we cannot afford to deny ourselves the love for which we were created. God is relentless in his openness so that we can fulfil our destiny – even though freedom to reject or ignore him is not denied.

Who are the poor and sick? Certainly Jesus found such people natural receivers of his call. But they can also stand for any of us, if we will abandon the clutter of our self-centred concerns and proud possessions, really so tawdry and distracting from the glory of God.

- Pray for readiness to receive God.
- Thank God for his simplicity and love.
- May we be spared from pushing God into second place.

PROPER 9

LUKE 15.1–7

Now all the tax-collectors and sinners were coming near to listen to Jesus. And the Pharisees and the scribes were grumbling and saying, 'This fellow welcomes sinners and eats with them.'

So he told them this parable: 'Which one of you, having a hundred sheep and losing one of them, does not leave the ninety-nine in the wilderness and go after the one that is lost until he finds it? When he has found it, he lays it on his shoulders and rejoices.

'And when he comes home, he calls together his friends and neighbours, saying to them, "Rejoice with me, for I have found my sheep that was lost."

'Just so, I tell you, there will be more joy in heaven over one sinner who repents than over ninety-nine righteous people who need no repentance.'

COMMENTARY

The story ends with a flick of the tail: there are of course no 'righteous persons who need no repentance' – and those who think they belong in that category only show how self-satisfied they are. No, we all stand in need of God's 'search' for us – and the message is that his love for each of us is such that he is relentless and unlimited in his quest for our loving response. We should note that in the world of Jesus, sheep are not 'cuddly', fluffy objects of sentiment but valued investments. Such are we in our creator's eyes – all of us, without exception; and there is no place for some thinking themselves better than others.

REFLECTION

Especially as we get older, we are very inclined to lose possessions, sometimes things that are particularly precious or useful to us. More seriously, we are more likely to 'lose' (as we put it) people who are precious to us. But here we can stick to material possessions, and we know full well the energy and worry, sometimes fretful, that we devote to our searches: of rooms, drawers and pockets.

Then (often!) comes the moment of finding and there is relief, and even remorse for the fuss we have made! The focus is all on the value of the lost item *to us* – for we know it well and we have invested something of ourselves in it. So the matter is very personal, and others may well mock us for the fuss we make – or at least find it difficult to comprehend. So we are precious to God, and are made for the most direct and simple relationship with him that we can imagine.

- Pray to dare to realize our value to God.

- Give thanks for the relentlessness of his 'search' for us.

- Pray for all who hide from the delight which is available to us.

PROPER 10

LUKE 15.11–24

Then Jesus said, 'There was a man who had two sons. The younger of them said to his father, "Father, give me the share of the property that will belong to me." So he divided his property between them.

'A few days later the younger son gathered all he had and travelled to a distant country, and there he squandered his property in dissolute living. When he had spent everything, a severe famine took place throughout that country, and he began to be in need.

'So he went and hired himself out to one of the citizens of that country, who sent him to his fields to feed the pigs. He would gladly have filled himself with the pods that the pigs were eating; and no one gave him anything.

'But when he came to himself he said, "How many of my father's hired hands have bread enough and to spare, but here I am dying of hunger! I will get up and go to my father, and I will say to him, 'Father, I have sinned against heaven and before you; I am no longer worthy to be called your son; treat me like one of your hired hands.'"

'So he set off and went to his father. But while he was still far off, his father saw him and was filled with compassion; he ran and put his arms around him and kissed him. Then the son said to him, "Father, I have sinned against heaven and before you; I am no longer worthy to be called your son."

'But the father said to his slaves, "Quickly, bring out a robe – the best one – and put it on him; put a ring on his finger and sandals on his feet. And get the fatted calf and kill it, and let us eat and celebrate; for this son of mine was dead and is alive again; he was lost and is found!" And they began to celebrate.'

COMMENTARY

We call it the story of the *prodigal* son, and it is a very moralistic way of looking at it – as if the point was to get us to disapprove of the wanton

90

behaviour of the young man. No, the focus of the parable is the love of the father, who goes to all lengths to reach out to the son as he returns. There is no enquiry into the son's exact motives, no laying down of conditions. The son's gesture of return is met by the father's absolute acceptance. And so it is, we are to understand, with ourselves and God. It is in truth the parable of the loving Father, and he is to be the focus of our attention and desire.

REFLECTION

There is of course more to this story, and it concerns the behaviour of the older son when the wanderer returns – and is welcomed. He is resentful and bitter. It is a situation that is not unknown, both in families and in Christian groups. And the older son's attitude – and its replica in life – is pernicious and intolerable. Within families such situations can rankle for a lifetime: so easily does love go out of the door, never to return, with far too much pride at stake.

There is no easy solution, except by determination to make love and acceptance the only guides to both heart and behaviour. Half-measures will not work – whether conditions of various kinds, or waiting for apologies, or standing on 'principle'.

In this sense God is not concerned with 'principles', but only with the thrust of our hearts, however muddled they may have been and may in part remain.

- Pray for the gift of openness to others.
- Look into yourself: how do you need still to 'return' to God?
- Thank God for so much 'welcome' already received.

PROPER 11

LUKE 19.1–10

Jesus entered Jericho and was passing through it. A man was there named Zacchaeus; he was a chief tax-collector and was rich. He was trying to see who Jesus was, but on account of the crowd he could not, because he was short in stature. So he ran ahead and climbed a sycomore tree to see Jesus, because he was going to pass that way.

When Jesus came to the place, he looked up and said to him, 'Zacchaeus, hurry and come down; for I must stay at your house today.' So he hurried down and was happy to welcome Jesus. All who saw it began to grumble and said, 'He has gone to be the guest of one who is a sinner.'

Zacchaeus stood there and said to the Lord, 'Look, half of my possessions, Lord, I will give to the poor; and if I have defrauded anyone of anything, I will pay back four times as much.'

Then Jesus said to him, 'Today salvation has come to this house, because he too is a son of Abraham. For the Son of Man came to seek out and to save the lost.'

COMMENTARY

The moving story of Zacchaeus is told only by Luke and is characteristic of Luke's picture of Jesus' mission. He came 'to seek out and save the lost'. And the hoarding of wealth, especially ill-gotten wealth, is among the clearest signs of being 'lost' – that is, being so wrapped up in one's possessions and so dependent on increasing them that one has no energy and no desire to attend either to God or to one's fellow human beings. The only cure is to rid oneself of these wrongly gained possessions. But the first step is to move in Jesus' direction. To let that happen makes the rest possible.

REFLECTION

Years ago there was a one-man show at a London theatre where an actor spoke Mark's Gospel from beginning to end by heart, which was quite a feat in itself. The night I was there, the only bit that caused clear disquiet among the middle-class audience was Jesus' words when he encounters a rich man who would like to follow him. Jesus tells him to sell the lot and give it away. Then: 'How hard it is for those who trust in wealth to enter the Kingdom of God!' People who took the story of Jesus' Passion in their stride were stung by those words, though nobody fled in panic.

Every trend in society, every instinct we have to protect ourselves and provide for our future and that of our families resists the force of this teaching of Jesus – and we leave it for another day, which we hope will never quite arrive. Yet it comes time and again in the Gospels: it is central, not marginal. The Church too, in its common life, is no example, for all the self-sacrifice and generosity of many individuals. But is it not a good cure for pride and complacency?

- Pray for a generous heart.
- Pray for the world's poor.
- Pray to grow in self-awareness before God.

PROPER 12

LUKE 12.1-7

Meanwhile, when the crowd gathered in thousands, so that they trampled on one another, he began to speak first to his disciples, 'Beware of the yeast of the Pharisees, that is, their hypocrisy. Nothing is covered up that will not be uncovered, and nothing secret that will not become known. Therefore whatever you have said in the dark will be heard in the light, and what you have whispered behind closed doors will be proclaimed from the housetops.

'I tell you, my friends, do not fear those who kill the body, and after that can do nothing more. But I will warn you whom to fear: fear him who, after he has killed, has authority to cast into hell. Yes, I tell you, fear him!

'Are not five sparrows sold for two pennies? Yet not one of them is forgotten in God's sight. But even the hairs of your head are all counted. Do not be afraid; you are of more value than many sparrows.'

COMMENTARY

This passage has more than one message, but all combine to urge us to honest assessment of ourselves before God. If we are his beloved creatures, how could we think it worthwhile to pretend to be what we are not? Such fantasy springs from insecurity – which God's love for us makes absurd, at the very deepest level. So: first, though there may be every reason for tact, there is no sense in hypocrisy and lack of openness, as long as we do not give pain. Similarly, we should not so value ourselves that we approach our fellows as threats to our well-being. Sometimes, they may be just that, but they have no final power over us. And this is because our value comes from God our creator whose love for us is without limit.

REFLECTION

How many secrets do you have? Some people cannot retain them at all: ask them to keep some secret, and you might as well print it in a newspaper or post it on a hoarding. But all of us have secrets of our very own that we rarely divulge to anyone. Some are too shaming, even if they refer to matters long past. Some are not so much shaming as embarrassing – habits or events or situations that we would prefer to forget and certainly do not want others to know about. Sometimes we keep our secrets out of modesty: we have no wish to brag about our successes or our virtues. We are not the type to tell everyone about the day we played for Manchester United. Other secrets have been entrusted to us by others, in the family or by good friends. We would no more reveal them than our own more personal secrets.

But before God neither deception nor even the keeping of confidences have any place: not because God is the 'all-seeing eye' or the super-spy to outdo all others, but because his love is such that our little attempts at secrecy lose all point. He forgives what shames us, makes our embarrassment fall away, and deals in the same way with those who have trusted us. The Kingdom of God is for love that needs no dark places, no pride.

- Pray to accept the openness that God brings.
- Give thanks for our infinite value in God's eyes.
- Pray to realize that love casts out fear.

PROPER 13

LUKE 6.20–23

Then he looked up at his disciples and said: 'Blessed are you who are poor, for yours is the kingdom of God.

'Blessed are you who are hungry now, for you will be filled.

'Blessed are you who weep now, for you will laugh.

'Blessed are you when people hate you, and when they exclude you, revile you, and defame you on account of the Son of Man.

'Rejoice on that day and leap for joy, for surely your reward is great in heaven; for that is what their ancestors did to the prophets.'

COMMENTARY

In Matthew 5 the more familiar version of the beatitudes is also the more 'religious': 'Blessed are the poor *in spirit* . . . those who hunger and thirst *for righteousness*'. Here, in Luke, they are more down to earth, closer to ordinary life and everyday experience. But they are in fact intensely spiritual in their own way: we are to reach God in the 'ordinary'. What is 'blessed' about being poor is that it may make us receivers of God's rule – for we can be free of worldly pride and ambition that can fill our horizon. And the hungry may (is this too idealistic?) be 'filled' by God's bounty, for emptiness of stomach makes us aware of the emptiness of our hearts. But there is no denying that the message is tough and wildly idealistic. But can that do us any harm?

REFLECTION

'Please, sir,' said the bright nuisance at the back of the class, 'does that mean that once God has filled you up and made you laugh, he no longer gives you his blessing or cares about you?' 'No, of course not,' says the brighter teacher, though even he has to think about a decent answer with some care. The fact is that when all goes well with us and we have everything we need for our well-being, we are all too inclined, whether we believe in God or not, to rest on our laurels, and to be self-satisfied, even smug. What, after all, do we actually *need* God for?

Jesus takes poverty, hunger, unhappiness and persecution as images for our true position as human creatures: without recognition of our need for God, our creator and source of all our good, we are ignoring the greatest and truest blessing of all – to be able to rest in the knowledge and love of him, our beginning and our ending. In the light of him, our present 'riches' will seem paltry, and we long for the riches of his glory, here already, once we open ourselves to the true scale of things.

- Pray for a right sense of the proportions of our lives.
- May we be open and ready for God's blessing.
- Pray for readiness to stand fast for the cause of faith.

PROPER 14

LUKE 6.32-36

'If you love those who love you, what credit is that to you? For even sinners love those who love them.

'If you do good to those who do good to you, what credit is that to you? For even sinners do the same.

'If you lend to those from whom you hope to receive, what credit is that to you? Even sinners lend to sinners, to receive as much again.

'But love your enemies, do good, and lend, expecting nothing in return. Your reward will be great, and you will be children of the Most High; for he is kind to the ungrateful and the wicked.

'Be merciful, just as your Father is merciful.'

COMMENTARY

As often, Jesus' teaching urges us to be transparent – not naïvely or simple-mindedly (though sometimes that is exactly what we need to be), but out of honesty and generosity before God. There is no point, no possible sense in pretence. We may even be taken for a ride, but that is a risk we must be prepared to take as part of being 'fools for Christ's sake'. There is nothing in all Jesus' teaching which is more against the grain than what we have in this passage, and we fail to get anywhere near it time and again. But, especially as we become older and less attached to dignity and pride, we can expand our vision – and at least get the feel of a wonderful world where life could be as Jesus paints it.

REFLECTION

'In all these eighty years', commented an older person to me, 'loving those who have done me wrong is the hardest Christian lesson of all.' So began a short conversation during worship about loving our enemies. We acknowledged that we have all got enemies – lots of people whom we actively hate rather than positively love. We reflected on the ways in which we try to make this command to be merciful, forgiving and generous, more manageable. One old man insisted that enemies can be loved if only we will try harder. Another attempted to spiritualize an interpretation of what it means to love an enemy. But when asked what this might mean in his attitude to his son-in-law, he exclaimed, 'Of course, I have forgiven him, but I'll never forget.'

What people of excuses we can be! How easily we try to reduce the demands of the passage. Yet surely we must look at the active, verbal character of these demands. Love in this passage is not a noun, a characteristic, an emotional state; it is an action. While it may be impossible to *feel* love for our enemies, it is not impossible to act in certain ways, even for those whom experience has shown to be the most entrenched of opponents. What Jesus means by the love of enemies becomes clear in three verbal demands: 'Do good', 'Bless' and 'Pray'.

This is a lifetime's work as we explore and uncover the ever-fresh depths of God's generosity. And finally at the end of this passage we are reminded that God's measure is not justice, but mercy. This is wonderfully good news both to live within and to act upon through our generous sharing.

- Reflect upon the generosity of God's understanding and forgiveness.
- Pray for those who have done you harm.
- Pray for the gift of love to help forgive others.

PROPER 15

LUKE 6.46–49

'Why do you call me "Lord, Lord", and do not do what I tell you? I will show you what someone is like who comes to me, hears my words, and acts on them.

'That one is like a man building a house, who dug deeply and laid the foundation on rock; when a flood arose, the river burst against that house but could not shake it, because it had been well built.

'But the one who hears and does not act is like a man who built a house on the ground without foundation. When the river burst against it, immediately it fell, and great was the ruin of that house.'

COMMENTARY

The message is crystal clear. There is for all of us a gap between what we believe in and even publicly stand for and what we live by in practice. And it is not just a matter of simple failure to live up to our principles; it is often more subtle – failures of imagination and discernment. What faith really points to in terms of life is not always in line with our deeply held religious prejudices! To have stuck all our lives to what we were taught (or what we fondly think we were taught) is no guarantee that we are building on rock. Jesus' leading is liable to be more flexible than we may care to imagine. Who can tell where he will take us next?

REFLECTION

Stark 'either/or' choices are all very well for preachers, as well as being convenient for the hearers: we can see what is being said to us, and there are few complexities to confuse us. At least, that is how it is until we move into what we know as 'the real world'. There, matters are nothing like so simple. We may start off on projects. As we go on, there are ups and downs. We dive and swerve. We are virtually compelled to cut corners in order to survive. So if our plans and our hopes began by being founded on rock (in the terms put before us), sand has got into those foundations. And it's scarcely a matter of 'sin' on our part (though it may be), more a matter of just the way things go.

In other words, the hard questions come when black and white are not the only colours on the palette. Then where do we stand before God? Well, we learn that a pure conscience is not any kind of guarantee. What *is* guaranteed is the love of God for us mediocre, wrong-headed creatures, victims of the world, as well as our own foolish ways. And will he not love and accept us, come what may?

- Pray for the gift of wise choice.

- Praise God for his unending mercies.

- Pray that we may know our need of God.

PROPER 16

LUKE 7.11–17

Soon afterwards Jesus went to a town called Nain, and his disciples and a large crowd went with him. As he approached the gate of the town, a man who had died was being carried out. He was his mother's only son, and she was a widow; and with her was a large crowd from the town.

When the Lord saw her, he had compassion for her and said to her, 'Do not weep.' Then he came forward and touched the bier, and the bearers stood still. And he said, 'Young man, I say to you, rise!' The dead man sat up and began to speak, and Jesus gave him to his mother.

Fear seized all of them; and they glorified God, saying, 'A great prophet has risen among us!' and 'God has looked favourably on his people!' This word about him spread throughout Judea and all the surrounding country.

COMMENTARY

We read the story of a supreme act of compassion: returning to the mother not only this love of her life but also her only bulwark against destitution. At all levels, it is the difference between life and death. But to the Christian reader this is not just the story of a great marvel; it is also a symptom of God's consistent priority – of which Jesus' Resurrection will be the supreme example and sign. Which has the last word where God is concerned, death or life? For many people, death has to be the answer. But the Christian message is that 'life' (however worked out) is always the final note. God is with us at every turn, bringing into being the great good that we call 'life' – in its many forms, amazing and unpredictable.

REFLECTION

We all know that in Europe (as distinct from almost everywhere else) Christianity is in a weak state – after centuries of strength. It is weak in numbers and influence, and often uncertain in belief. About no subject is this truer than death. We are unusual in that not only unbelievers but also a proportion of Christians are at best hazy about life after death. At the same time, many people, including most Christians, set great store, both by their own survival and by reunion with their loved ones after death, and they feel in touch with them in the here and now. Others engage in spiritualist practices of one kind or another. Little of all this may have anything to do with God.

The perspective of Jesus on these things is very different from ours. In the first place, we are to abandon our lives, readily and totally, in the service of God's cause. We must not cling to our lives, following our own interest. At the same time, we must be eager to receive whatever God our creator and life-giver has in store for us – beyond our imagining. In other words, to save yourself you must throw yourself away, in whatever way life and your inner heart leads you to do it. The future is not in our hands at all, but in the hands of God, our loving life-giver and saviour.

- Pray to live and die for the Kingdom of God.

- Pray for faith in God our life-giver.

- We thank God always for the gift of his abundant life.

PROPER 17

LUKE 8.22–25

One day Jesus got into a boat with his disciples, and he said to them, 'Let us go across to the other side of the lake.' So they put out, and while they were sailing he fell asleep. A gale swept down on the lake, and the boat was filling with water, and they were in danger.

They went to him and woke him up, shouting, 'Master, Master, we are perishing!' And he woke up and rebuked the wind and the raging waves; they ceased, and there was a calm.

He said to them, 'Where is your faith?'

They were afraid and amazed, and said to one another, 'Who then is this, that he commands even the winds and the water, and they obey him?'

COMMENTARY

It is a story full of symbolism – more important, for what it stands for than for its literal content. The Bible makes much of the dangers of water, whether sea or lake: think of Noah and Jonah, as well as Psalms 107 and 130. With the Mediterranean near to hand and internal 'seas' closer still, Jesus and his followers could react readily to the terror of water and the importance of mastering its riotous tendencies. Here, it serves to bring out (as the Old Testament passages also do) the need for trusting in God. The symbol moves easily into giving us a lesson in the fact that our 'survival' with God is, in a way, always by the skin of our teeth: less alarmingly, it is not that we deserve his love or have a right to it – it is always by his grace alone. And is that not always the case with true love?

REFLECTION

'We are perishing.' The cry might come from a huge proportion of the inhabitants of the world (and in one sense could come from all of us, as a statement of plain fact). Here, it is a sign of panic. And, whether in panic or despair or not, all of us have episodes in our lives where 'I am perishing' is a reaction that feels forced upon us.

It may seem facile to say, 'Well, read the story, all you need do is turn to Christ, and you will be rescued'; though many Christians believe it and act upon it, while many other Christians lose faith or are bewildered because the disaster takes its inexorable course; and still other believers muddle their way through as best they can. But truly it is a matter of the level at which divine rescue operates. Too often we wish it would operate at the level that is most obviously convenient for us, regardless of the rules and the mechanisms of the created order.

The story, however, is an image, a metaphor, and what is at stake is not shipwrecks or famine or cancer, but the dependence on God which we must cultivate in the depth of our lives, come what may, regardless of the perils that beset us. Jesus calms the storm but endured the Cross – and reigns.

- Pray for a deeper reliance on God.
- May we learn to love God, come what may.
- Pray never to evade the more difficult demands of faith.

PROPER 18

1 CORINTHIANS 13.1–7

If I speak in the tongues of mortals and of angels, but do not have love, I am a noisy gong or a clanging cymbal.

And if I have prophetic powers, and understand all mysteries and all knowledge, and if I have all faith, so as to remove mountains, but do not have love, I am nothing.

If I give away all my possessions, and if I hand over my body so that I may boast, but do not have love, I gain nothing.

Love is patient; love is kind; love is not envious or boastful or arrogant or rude. It does not insist on its own way; it is not irritable or resentful; it does not rejoice in wrongdoing, but rejoices in the truth.

It bears all things, believes all things, hopes all things, endures all things.

COMMENTARY

In a long section of this first letter to the new Christian community in the Greek city of Corinth, Paul turns to their own internal relations and how they esteem one another, especially for their different styles of what we may call religious expertise (1 Corinthians 12–14). There are those who are much attached to the more spectacular ways of being religious: they babble wildly – and it is the Spirit speaking through *them*; they have insights not disclosed to others – and it is God favouring *them* with his deeper truth. These are phenomena which emerge from time to time in Christianity (and indeed in other faiths too). In chapter 13 (*not* written specially for today's weddings!) Paul seeks to put things into perspective. However admirable these happenings may be, they are useless in themselves. And they have no special virtue by comparison with the humbler Christian gifts (in church life, making the tea, cleaning the church). Love alone is to be the uniting bond among Christians and it is the prince of virtues.

REFLECTION

In recent years there has been a huge spread of the more vivid styles of Christian worship. No doubt it is in part a reaction against the staid and over-formal character of much worship in the preceding period. Many of us can recall hours spent in dreary services, routine sermons – no wonder churchgoing has declined in many parts of Europe in particular.

St Paul was not wholly opposed to those exciting styles of worship as they showed themselves among some of his converts. But he was clear that love is far more important – and not always found where the more 'fizzy' styles of religion thrive. Love may not always be exciting, because it demands going against the grain of our selfish desires or needs. In other words, love goes with sacrifice, with a readiness to give ourselves generously in matters great and small. Only such a way of life – typified by Jesus – leads us to that relationship with God which is our true destiny.

- Pray for the gift of generous love, both to bestow and to receive.

- May worship be both heartfelt and thoughtful.

- Pray to rejoice in the truth.

PROPER 19

1 CORINTHIANS 13.8–13

Love never ends. But as for prophecies, they will come to an end; as for tongues, they will cease; as for knowledge, it will come to an end.

For we know only in part, and we prophesy only in part; but when the complete comes, the partial will come to an end.

When I was a child, I spoke like a child, I thought like a child, I reasoned like a child; when I became an adult, I put an end to childish ways.

For now we see in a mirror, dimly, but then we will see face to face. Now I know only in part; then I will know fully, even as I have been fully known.

And now faith, hope, and love abide, these three; and the greatest of these is love.

COMMENTARY

Paul will not pander to the pride of those Christians who seem to have special spiritual gifts – whether powerful preaching (which is what 'prophecy' means here), or speaking with tongues (seen as a sign of the Holy Spirit). Such gifts no doubt have their value, but they are only transient, and one day their time will reach its end. It will be as if they belonged to a Christian's immaturity. When we go beyond that stage, their passing value will be clear, and we shall know what truly counts. It is as if at present we see in a mirror (in Paul's day, far from clear) and one day we shall see 'face to face' – with the total clarity of God. And we shall realize what really counts: faith, hope – and love, the supreme virtue of the Christian life, now and for ever.

REFLECTION

'Being known' by anyone, let alone by God, is an uncertain matter. Partly we love it and long for it, at any rate as far as perhaps only a short list of people goes; but partly we are terrified and affronted by any such possibility. And in a sizeable number of us, the prospect of being known, *really* known, by anyone on any terms and to any degree at all remains appalling.

But is the thought of being known by God in a different category? For some, it makes things worse: who wants a snooping God? What would it say for human freedom? But we cannot truly understand what is involved, without introducing the fact of love, both God's and our own. God's love for us, his creatures, is unconditional – so Jesus teaches. So no place for fear, no place for reticence, and no sense in them either. Not because God is the greatest spy ever known, but because his love takes the whole matter to a different level. And, of course, we know its reliable shadow in our earthly loving. When that loving is at its best, there may still be secrets – things about us that are unknown to our partner (also things unknown to ourselves!) but they do not signify, for love abides.

- Pray to accept our maturity, given by God.

- Thank God that we are loved totally for our own sake; by God and those with whom we live in trust.

- Pray for gifts of faith, hope and love.

PROPER 20

PHILIPPIANS 4.4–9

Rejoice in the Lord always; again I will say, Rejoice. Let your gentleness be known to everyone. The Lord is near. Do not worry about anything, but in everything by prayer and supplication with thanksgiving let your requests be made known to God.

And the peace of God, which surpasses all understanding, will guard your hearts and your minds in Christ Jesus.

Finally, beloved, whatever is true, whatever is honourable, whatever is just, whatever is pure, whatever is pleasing, whatever is commendable, if there is any excellence and if there is anything worthy of praise, think about these things.

Keep on doing the things that you have learned and received and heard and seen in me, and the God of peace will be with you.

COMMENTARY

It is hard not to hum the familiar anthem by Henry Purcell, using the opening section of this passage. The passage comes from the deeply felt final part of Paul's letter that was written during one of his times in prison for his Christian activities; and he writes from the heart to the Christians in Philippi, a church he had founded and with whom he had the warmest relations. So he feels free to urge them to follow his example – and presses God's peace, with its richness of meaning, into their lives, summing up all virtues to which they aspire. And everything is in the context of Christ himself: 'The Lord is near.'

REFLECTION

This is probably the first bit of Paul ever to be familiar to me. It often appeared as the reading at assemblies at my secondary school. I guess it was our headmaster's favourite, and perhaps he hoped chiefly to inspire us to be honourable, just and pure. Compared to much of what Paul wrote, this passage is remarkable for its simplicity and straightforward beauty. No doubt it appealed for this reason too.

But perhaps it is not just about moral exhortation. What about the urging of readers to 'rejoice in the Lord'? Morally worthy people have been known to be less successful in developing the basic Christian confidence in God that lies behind these words. And note, it is confidence that can survive adverse circumstances: Paul was in prison, perhaps facing execution. In that case, the calm of this passage is astonishing – and it humbles us. It goes beyond the virtues that the average schoolboy can aspire to.

- Pray to get to the heart of God's peace.

- Seek to pray in a spirit of confident peace.

- Thank God for the high ideals that Scripture puts before us.

PROPER 21

EPHESIANS 6.10–17

Finally, be strong in the Lord and in the strength of his power. Put on the whole armour of God, so that you may be able to stand against the wiles of the devil.

For our struggle is not against enemies of blood and flesh, but against the rulers, against the authorities, against the cosmic powers of this present darkness, against the spiritual forces of evil in the heavenly places.

Therefore take up the whole armour of God, so that you may be able to withstand on that evil day, and having done everything, to stand firm. Stand therefore, and fasten the belt of truth around your waist, and put on the breastplate of righteousness.

As shoes for your feet put on whatever will make you ready to proclaim the gospel of peace. With all of these, take the shield of faith, with which you will be able to quench all the flaming arrows of the evil one.

Take the helmet of salvation, and the sword of the Spirit, which is the word of God.

COMMENTARY

There are Old Testament passages that point to many of the military metaphors that mark this passage, and the writer has concentrated them together to make a total picture of the Christian as a warrior. It has of course had a great history since Ephesians was written, some of it now seemingly regrettable. The intention is to bring out the serious element of struggle that belongs to Christian allegiance. If that element is absent, it is likely that we are failing to take our faith seriously – for there are opposing pressures in ourselves as well as in the outside world, which often fly in the face of the Christian picture of life as it should be. No good can come from pretending it is not so.

REFLECTION

In the later years of the nineteenth century, Great Britain had a long period of what was felt as peace. No European wars involved us: *our* wars were at a safe distance, in Africa or Asia. It might seem odd (or was it a strange kind of compensation?) that the churches chose at this time to develop military-style organizations for young people: the Boys' and Girls' Brigades and the Church Lads' Brigade, among others, complete with bands, flags, marching, even (artificial) weapons. And of course passages like our reading were a kind of inspiration. Also, hymns such as 'Onward, Christian Soldiers!' came into being.

All this now scarcely survives, except in a few places; and, of course, the Salvation Army, a special case in many ways. What's more, to many Christians, all this kind of behaviour and thinking strikes a most unfortunate note. We are people of peace, of love for enemies, and we should not confuse the issue, even if innocently.

Well, it makes for a worthwhile discussion, and we can enter into it with gusto!

- Pray for the gift of using the images in Scripture wisely.
- Pray to engage fearlessly in the battle against evil – in ourselves and in the world around us.

PROPER 22

COLOSSIANS 3.1–4

*So, if you have been raised with Christ, seek the things that are above,
where Christ is, seated at the right hand of God.*

*Set your minds on things that are above, not on things that are on
earth, for you have died, and your life is hidden with Christ in God.*

*When Christ who is your life is revealed, then you also will be revealed
with him in glory.*

COMMENTARY

These words are one of the strongest statements of the dramatic results
of Christ's Resurrection for his people. The first result concerns our
whole framework of life: we are 'raised' with him. Not simply as
individuals but as a community; we both belong together and have our
true being in relation to him – the centre and mainspring of our
existence. This does, all the same, mean effort and aspiring on our part:
we must still seek 'the things that are above' and go for making them
our own. And whatever the future holds, our destiny is wholly bound up
with Christ who binds us to God and to one another.

REFLECTION

There are many situations in life that are partly of the present and partly
of the future. Before a marriage, much of the future (almost all of it) is
already in position. Before a new job or a new school we live, to some
degree, in the partly known future. When we are moving into a new
house, at least the familiar furniture of the old one will be there
greeting us, some of it perhaps boring us to distraction.

The Christian life has always had something of this character. Much of
what God has to give his people is already ours: 'You *have been raised
with Christ.*' We have assurance, we have a settled relationship with our
creator and saviour: so there can be no fear, no worry – whatever may
then happen to us. But nevertheless: 'Set your minds on things that are

above! That is, we still have things to strive for, alternatives and pitfalls to avoid. And no doubt our mood and outlook will vary from one aspect to the other – from assurance to perplexity that spurs us to strive. But the ultimate future that is promised, that may seem extravagant and beyond all reasonable possibility, alone makes full sense of what is already ours. We live between times – and wedding day, moving day are always on the horizon, beckoning, partly known yet in another way unknown.

- Pray never to undervalue the place we have with God.
- Let us look forward with delight to what God has in store.
- Give thanks for God's life given to us.

PROPER 23

MATTHEW 5.43–48

Jesus said, 'You have heard that it was said, "You shall love your neighbour and hate your enemy."

'But I say to you, Love your enemies and pray for those who persecute you, so that you may be children of your Father in heaven; for he makes his sun rise on the evil and on the good, and sends rain on the righteous and on the unrighteous.

'For if you love those who love you, what reward do you have? Do not even the tax-collectors do the same?

'And if you greet only your brothers and sisters, what more are you doing than others? Do not even the Gentiles do the same?

'Be perfect, therefore, as your heavenly Father is perfect.'

COMMENTARY

It is not possible to find a candid equivalent in Jewish teaching, for the command to love our enemy, that might have been inherited by both Jesus and Matthew. However, we do hear sobering and moving stories from down the centuries of Christians who sought to obey it, contrary though it is to our natural tendency. Here, it is not simply stated, it is also explained and reasons are given. All of us, whether we get on with one another or not, live in the same world and all are equally creatures of God. In that way, more unites us all than can possibly separate us. To relate only to those like ourselves cannot seriously count as a virtuous achievement, after all! Anyway, as Jesus' own, we are required to be no less than perfect. The goal, stated so boldly, makes us gasp.

REFLECTION

It *might* be offensive to give examples, but in a great many societies, 'enemies' are a fixed and inherited commodity: there's 'us' and there's 'them'. Having any kind of love for the other lot is as unlikely as pigs flying. But in the greater part of English society these days, 'enemies' are fairly difficult to find, or at any rate to admit to. There's no war that is close at hand. We may have groups that we do not naturally associate with, but to call them our enemies is much too strong. Now, we would be more likely to say that we wish nobody any harm, that we are peace-loving and would help anybody (what, *anybody*?) in a difficulty or bother. It's true that further enquiry may reveal the school bully or the insufferable workmate, but we have our ways of avoiding them and our belief in our own basic loving kindness remains – really, a fashionable point of pride. But often this feeling is not very deep and whether it amounts to what you could call 'love' for opponents and those different from ourselves – well, that may be another matter.

As for being 'perfect', that is something else – and we should hesitate to claim we had got there! But it is our destiny that our characters should be mirrors of God's own. Is that beyond our hope?

- Pray to resist limiting our goodness to others.

- May we aim high in the quest for God.

- Pray to recognize God's gift of impossible ideals.

PROPER 24

MATTHEW 6.1-4

[Jesus said to the disciples,] 'Beware of practising your piety before others in order to be seen by them; for then you have no reward from your Father in heaven.

'So whenever you give alms, do not sound a trumpet before you, as the hypocrites do in the synagogues and in the streets, so that they may be praised by others. Truly I tell you, they have received their reward.

'But when you give alms, do not let your left hand know what your right hand is doing, so that your alms may be done in secret; and your Father who sees in secret will reward you.'

COMMENTARY

Religious people have temptations all their own. It is to be hoped we can laugh at ourselves for it, but it is very easy to feel smug when, for example, we are particularly (or perhaps even not that!) generous with our money or with our churchgoing. In the opening part of chapter 6, Matthew gives the teaching of Jesus on each of the three chief devotional practices in Jewish life: prayer, fasting and almsgiving. Christians have inherited these, and Jesus gives the same lesson for all three: no showing off, no self-regard, no false exaggeration, eyes directed solely to God for whose love alone we engage in the practice of our religion, whoever we are.

REFLECTION

If it is corrupt to be generous in order to win people's praise, it may seem even more so to do it with an eye on rewards from God. Surely we should give money and goods away simply because it is the right thing to do: only then can we think of purity of heart and mind. We are not even, of course, to enjoy a private warm glow as we make our secret donations.

Yet this way of thinking may seem a bit too austere. There is perhaps something more to be said for attending to the reward that God promises. It is, we know, quite different from earthly rewards such as approval from those around us or plaques on walls or our name on published lists of benefactors. God's only reward for us is the fullness of his own love. Perfection of relationship with him is our true destiny; and our little earthly virtues, practised modestly and without afterthoughts, go to make that relationship our natural next and final step. It is less a 'reward' in the earthly sense than the destined outcome, following as night follows day. Not a payback but an outcome.

- Pray for purity of motive in all our dealings.
- May love for God be our overriding aim.
- Thank God for his abundant generosity.

PROPER 25

MATTHEW 6.19–24

Jesus said, 'Do not store up for yourselves treasures on earth, where moth and rust consume and where thieves break in and steal; but store up for yourselves treasures in heaven, where neither moth nor rust consumes and where thieves do not break in and steal. For where your treasure is, there your heart will be also.

'The eye is the lamp of the body. So, if your eye is healthy, your whole body will be full of light; but if your eye is unhealthy, your whole body will be full of darkness. If then the light in you is darkness, how great is the darkness!

'No one can serve two masters: for a slave will either hate the one and love the other, or be devoted to the one and despise the other. You cannot serve God and wealth.'

COMMENTARY

Nothing reveals the true direction of our loyalties and our hopes so clearly as our attitude to our money and property. Even if we are not obsessed by the determination to increase our wealth, most of us are likely to be keen to hold on to most of what we have. It follows that wealth is the great test of the depth of our love for God. There are of course ways of possessing without being attached in one's heart: ways too of acquiring without greed and using our wealth with sacrificial generosity, but most of us in the modern Western world, perhaps especially those who have the seriousness to embrace the Christian life, are likely to have this as a nagging weakness, the point where we can afford no complacency.

REFLECTION

If you were asked to describe a successful person, what would you say? What does a successful person look like? Compare the possible answers from a child with the whole of their life ahead of them, and an older person with much of their life behind them. I wonder how different their answers might be?

No doubt we measure success in all kinds of different ways – our houses or cars or other material possessions that we surround ourselves with. But for others the mark of such a successful person might be to be recognized, respected and honoured by the community for the way in which they have lived their lives and the contribution that they have made to others. One of the great gifts of old age is that life changes our perspective so that we value spiritual things as well as physical needs.

So often success is described in our culture in terms of material possessions. Material things are very important to us. The question, however, is: What do things say about us? Do material things say anything about us? Some people would argue that things say nothing about people. What do you think? Perhaps things do say a great deal about us. I remember someone saying, 'Money talks – it says bye-bye.' But money says more than that. What does it say about you?

One of the most important things that money says about us has to do with our heart's allegiance. When money talks, it tells where your heart is. So the real question here is that we need to consider where our heart is. True success in God's eyes has everything to do with where our heart is. Success is shaped by the condition of our hearts.

- Pray for those who nurture the dreams and ambitions of young people.
- Thank God for the wisdom that old age brings.
- Pray for a balanced perspective on life, money and success.

BIBLE SUNDAY

JOHN 5.36–47

Jesus said: 'The works that the Father has given me to complete, the very works that I am doing, testify on my behalf that the Father has sent me. And the Father who sent me has himself testified on my behalf. You have never heard his voice or seen his form, and you do not have his word abiding in you, because you do not believe him whom he has sent.

'You diligently study the scriptures because you think that in them you have eternal life, and it is they that testify on my behalf. Yet you refuse to come to me to have life. I do not accept glory from human beings. But I know that you do not have the love of God in you. I have come in my Father's name, and you do not accept me; if another comes in his own name, you will accept him. How can you believe when you accept glory from one another and do not seek the glory that comes from the one who alone is God?

'Do not think that I will accuse you before the Father; your accuser is Moses, on whom you have set your hope. If you believed Moses, you would believe me, for he wrote about me. But if you do not believe what he wrote, how will you believe what I say?'

COMMENTARY

The Bible is a very big book! It is always best to have in mind that it is a collection of books, written over a long period of time. And they are books of many different kinds: laws, histories, letters, Gospels – to name only a few. However these various writings started life, they came together finally under the auspices of the Christian Church – because, in many different ways, they were read as throwing light on Jesus our Lord and bearing witness to him. In other words, when we celebrate the Bible, it is because it is one of the ways in which we celebrate Jesus. And we celebrate him because he shows us truth about God and leads us to him.

REFLECTION

The experience we have of the Bible varies much. For some, it is heard only in church, in short sections, which may or may not be explained by the preacher. For many, if it exists at all, it is as an unopened book at home or perhaps only in hotel rooms. For a few, it is a daily source of strength and inspiration; and some have learnt about it and realize that its different parts must be read in their contexts – it is not helpful to plough through it in ignorance or to read it at random – the part you choose may or may not prove helpful.

We call the Bible the 'word of God', but all of it comes to us by way of a multitude of human voices, telling its stories to their families and friends; and human hands, writing its various books down over many years; and then used by countless Christians down the centuries all over the world, for their spiritual good.

At the same time, it mediates God to us, alongside the Christian community and the sacraments, and we, with our fellow Christians, read it as a springboard for prayer and action.

• Pray to use the Bible thoughtfully and carefully as God's gift.

• Pray to be open to God's word as part of our Christian nourishment.

ALL SAINTS

MATTHEW 5.1–12

When Jesus saw the crowds, he went up the mountain; and after he sat down, his disciples came to him. Then he began to speak, and taught them, saying:

'Blessed are the poor in spirit, for theirs is the kingdom of heaven.

'Blessed are those who mourn, for they will be comforted.

'Blessed are the meek, for they will inherit the earth.

'Blessed are those who hunger and thirst for righteousness, for they will be filled.

'Blessed are the merciful, for they will receive mercy.

'Blessed are the pure in heart, for they will see God.

'Blessed are the peacemakers, for they will be called children of God.

'Blessed are those who are persecuted for righteousness' sake, for theirs is the kingdom of heaven.

'Blessed are you when people revile you and persecute you and utter all kinds of evil against you falsely on my account.

'Rejoice and be glad, for your reward is great in heaven, for in the same way they persecuted the prophets who were before you.'

COMMENTARY

The eight beatitudes open the Sermon on the Mount, the great core of Jesus' teaching as given in the Gospel of Matthew (5–7). The subject is life in the Kingdom of God which Jesus comes to proclaim. In these brief statements, we see outlined the key features of the Christian character. Those who attain this style of life, with these preferences to the fore in both mind and deed, will certainly receive God's 'blessing' – the seal and endorsement of his love. The first of the eight is perhaps the hardest to understand: one attempt to be clearer said, 'Blessed are those who know their need of God' – that is, who can abandon all pride and pretence before God. We may see this as basic to all the other qualities and courses of life that we are to pursue.

REFLECTION

There is a discussion from time to time over whether it is a good thing to single out certain people as 'saints', in former times or now; or whether we should recognize that in vital ways all Christians are God's holy people, set aside for his purpose of love and equal in his sight. In the New Testament, the word 'saints' or 'holy people' is used in this second way, emphasizing our common calling and the gift we all share in Christ.

Nevertheless, within this basic setting, there seems much to be said for taking strength and encouragement from people of the past and present whose lives have shown heroic devotion to God's cause. In them, we can look for Christ's special image and be moved to stronger faith and love in our own lives. There will, of course, be some formally designated saints, whom we do not find particularly congenial or inspiring, perhaps for good reasons – they lived in times so different from our own. But others are men and women we chime in with: they encourage and fortify us, and we are glad of their fellowship.

- Pray to grow in devotion to God in and through his holy ones.

- Thank God for those who, not dissimilar to ourselves, have shown heroic love for him and for those around them.

PROPER 26/
FOURTH SUNDAY
BEFORE ADVENT

MATTHEW 6.25–34

Jesus said to his disciples: 'Therefore I tell you, do not worry about your life, what you will eat or what you will drink, or about your body, what you will wear. Is not life more than food, and the body more than clothing?

'Look at the birds of the air; they neither sow nor reap nor gather into barns, and yet your heavenly Father feeds them. Are you not of more value than they? And can any of you by worrying add a single hour to your span of life?

'And why do you worry about clothing? Consider the lilies of the field, how they grow; they neither toil nor spin, yet I tell you, even Solomon in all his glory was not clothed like one of these.

'But if God so clothes the grass of the field, which is alive today and tomorrow is thrown into the oven, will he not much more clothe you – you of little faith?

'Therefore do not worry, saying, "What will we eat?" or "What will we drink?" or "What will we wear?" For it is the Gentiles who strive for all these things; and indeed your heavenly Father knows that you need all these things.

'But strive first for the kingdom of God and his righteousness, and all these things will be given to you as well. So do not worry about tomorrow, for tomorrow will bring worries of its own. Today's trouble is enough for today.'

COMMENTARY

This passage is beautiful to our ears and even our imagination, but it will strike most who hear it as hopelessly impractical. Worse, to behave in the way recommended is surely foolhardy and irresponsible. Worse still, it will only mean that we have to be picked up by others, or else, in modern Europe at least, by the state. What can be the good of that? Perhaps we have to say that this is a vision of life that belongs to the heady youth of the Christian movement: and maybe it was already scarcely practical when the evangelist wrote it down in his book some 50 years after the lifetime of Jesus. On the other hand, if a Christian does not have impossible ideals and hopes, how is it possible to make gestures – at least – that show the priority of God in our life and in the choices that we make? After all, 'tomorrow' is not what we live for: God's 'day' is the constant 'now'.

REFLECTION

I have been trying to think of people I have known whom these words describe, and who live by this teaching – for example, certain members of the Franciscan order. But even for them, a treasurer hovers in the background and they do not lack for basic provision. Others I think of are often a puzzle in our society and are picked up by their friends when their improvidence and carefree generosity lands them in real difficulties.

But none of this spoils the worth of the ideal depicted in this passage. Perhaps what is chiefly at stake is our choice of priorities: 'strive *first* for the kingdom of God'. For most people, including many of Christian allegiance, this is a genuine challenge; for 'seek the kingdom *when convenient*' or 'when other matters have been secured' represent the active ideals. After all, we have duties to our families and their future provision. Prudence is after all one of the classic virtues, before Christianity was ever thought of. But, there is something reckless about following Jesus: can we deny it?

- Pray for the gift of courage in our discipleship.

- Pray for the gift of right judgement as we face our daily demands.

PROPER 27/
THIRD SUNDAY
BEFORE ADVENT

MARK 4.30-34

Jesus said, 'With what can we compare the kingdom of God, or what parable will we use for it?

'It is like a mustard seed, which, when sown upon the ground, is the smallest of all the seeds on earth; yet when it is sown it grows up and becomes the greatest of all shrubs, and puts forth large branches, so that the birds of the air can make nests in its shade.'

With many such parables he spoke the word to them, as they were able to hear it; he did not speak to them except in parables, but he explained everything in private to his disciples.

COMMENTARY

Many of Jesus' parables aim to show us the character of the 'Kingdom of God' – so that we can learn the nature of the life that is asked of us, or rather of the life that we are invited to share. Here, we learn that if we enter the kingdom that Jesus plants in the world, we are certainly backing a winner! God's cause will not fail and we shall share in its success. Of course we can trust in God's ultimate triumph and keep our eyes open for the signs of the Kingdom all around us – and not always where we might expect. We may also notice that the words to describe the Kingdom will not always be what we are used to: 'parable' here means puzzling sayings or stories which demand our whole attention if we are to grasp their meaning. For God's 'meaning' both illuminates us and escapes us at the same time.

REFLECTION

New enterprises, whether in business or religion or any other human undertaking, often begin with high hopes and grand ambitions. Often people would not embark if they did not see a prospect of big conquests. Sometimes, of course, such hopes are disappointed or at least are gradually modified in the light of realities. Some good has been done, a measure of success has been achieved, but not really on the grand scale that marked the original hope.

All this is partly true of the Christian movement which Jesus initiated. From one point of view its success has been huge: it has spread throughout the world, often pervading society from top to bottom (though sometimes, as in much of Europe, receding in due course); and it has been as large-scale an influence on human life as any that has ever been. All the same, it continues to look forward rather than to rest on its laurels. The Kingdom of God is always both with us and yet beyond our grasp. Our prayer remains: 'May thy Kingdom come.'

- Pray for the coming of God's Kingdom.

- Reflect on your spiritual ambitions.

- Pray that your faith community may shape life with the values of the Kingdom.

PROPER 28/
SECOND SUNDAY
BEFORE ADVENT

MARK 3.1–6

*Again [Jesus] entered the synagogue, and a man was there who had a
withered hand. They watched him to see whether he would cure him on
the sabbath, so that they might accuse him.*

*And he said to the man who had the withered hand, 'Come forward.'
Then he said to them, 'Is it lawful to do good or to do harm on the
sabbath, to save life or to kill?,' but they were silent.*

*He looked around at them with anger; he was grieved at their hardness
of heart and said to the man, 'Stretch out your hand.' He stretched it
out, and his hand was restored.*

*The Pharisees went out and immediately conspired with the Herodians
against him, how to destroy him.*

COMMENTARY

In a literal way, the story does not really make convincing sense and
Jesus' behaviour seems perverse. The disease from which the man suffers
is crippling but it is in no ordinary sense of the word an emergency. To
wait till Sabbath ends will not materially affect his health. So Jesus is
waving a banner for a cause: love for the needy must take precedence
even over venerable customs and rules, such as the law that governs the
keeping of the Sabbath for orthodox Jews. As we know, the abandoning
of the basic traditional marks of Jewishness, of which the Sabbath was
one, was one of Paul's crucial moves when it came to making converts
of non-Jews. So a story like this, from the life of Jesus himself, gave
authority to such a policy. Jesus did not see observances of this sort as
binding when the call of the Kingdom was at stake. Its urgency gives it
right of way.

REFLECTION

We sometimes have a problem about when to stand up for our principles: and people differ on how ready they are to mount the ramparts or pick up a weapon. If you are the peaceable sort, you can easily land up betraying what you believe in as the key moment passes. If you are more inclined to leap rapidly to pick up a cudgel, you may cause more harm than good. It is not always easy to know when the moment for action has come.

When our faith comes into the picture, such decisions can be all the more painful. We do not want either to let our deepest loyalties be betrayed or to cause useless hostility. So we have to put our beliefs and views into some sort of order of value. Surely, we have to think carefully before we decide what really matters for the cause of God's truth.

- Pray for the grace to discern when we need to stand up for the cause of God.

- May we never lack courage to judge aright.

CHRIST THE KING

MARK 9.2–8

Six days later, Jesus took with him Peter and James and John, and led them up a high mountain apart, by themselves. And he was transfigured before them, and his clothes became dazzling white, such as no one on earth could bleach them.

And there appeared to them Elijah with Moses, who were talking with Jesus.

Then Peter said to Jesus, 'Rabbi, it is good for us to be here; let us make three dwellings, one for you, one for Moses, and one for Elijah.' He did not know what to say, for they were terrified.

Then a cloud overshadowed them, and from the cloud there came a voice, 'This is my Son, the Beloved; listen to him!'

Suddenly when they looked around, they saw no one with them any more, but only Jesus.

COMMENTARY

The theme of Christ the King is not without its complications. Popular hymns take it in their stride, and so do the language of devotion and the conventions of Christian art. The aim of today's celebration is of course to enforce the message that Christians place the authority of Christ – what he stood for and what he asks of us – above all other powers to which we may be subject. *Their* claims often seem to dominate life, in some societies more than others, but the authority of Christ has the sanction of our creator and our ultimate Lord, God himself. The story of the Transfiguration of Jesus in the presence of his disciples is designed to assure us that, despite all normal appearances and despite the Cross that begins to loom, Jesus' authority is supreme and inviolable. He is greater than even the great ones of old Israel who brought God's older guidance to his people.

REFLECTION

Current British attitudes to authority are so complex as to discourage analysis. Many people have little respect for traditional authorities and keep out of their way as much as they possibly can. A good many, including those in this first category, complain with vigour about alleged authorities while at the same time doing everything possible to frustrate their proper activities. At the personal level, therapists will often make a bee-line for authority figures and the impression they made, including their long-term legacy, for good or ill, whether parents, teachers or even partners – let alone employers, dominant friends and figures in churches.

But what about God as an authority figure? At first sight, it's straightforward. If we believe in him seriously, then is he not the greatest authority of all? There is no evading him, surely; and may not he be as destructive for us as perhaps people in our families have been? For few of us are wholly unscathed. Then we attend to Jesus: vulnerable and, in life and death, powerless. He then can mature us, for he does not – cannot – threaten us. And we learn that the path of simple love is the key: no strident assertion, or even quiet defensive barrier-building; neither any passive acquiescence in things as they are. Open love will show us both ourselves and God.

- Pray for the maturing influence of love.

- Pray for those who exercise authority in your life.

- Pray for those who make decisions over the lives of others.

APPENDIX

PRESENTATION OF CHRIST IN THE TEMPLE/ CANDLEMAS (2 FEBRUARY)

LUKE 2.27–32

Guided by the Spirit, Simeon came into the temple; and when the parents brought in the child Jesus, to do for him what was customary under the law, Simeon took him in his arms and praised God, saying, 'Master, now you are dismissing your servant in peace, according to your word; for my eyes have seen your salvation, which you have prepared in the presence of all peoples, a light for revelation to the Gentiles and for glory to your people Israel.'

COMMENTARY

The opening chapters of Luke's Gospel keep returning to the Jerusalem Temple. It is as if he wants to insist that we do not lose sight of the roots of Jesus (and of his work) in Israel, its scriptures and institutions. We all get our significance in part from our roots; and Luke sees Jesus' roots as given by God. So Simeon represents the best in old Israel and voices its mission and its hopes, now concentrated in the figure of the infant Jesus. His role is universal, going beyond the bounds of Israel to the whole human race. No wonder that the passage is linked with a festival of light.

REFLECTION

Whether it is a matter of class, race, religion or political loyalty, most of us have limits to our sympathies, groups who are not quite 'one of us'. I was once in a restaurant with a friend who cleared neighbouring tables by announcing: 'I don't like Catholics, Jews, Americans or Tories, but I do very much like blacks.' He was only a quarter serious, but all of us have points where mild prejudice goes solid: we probably deal with them politely but all the same the sign goes up: 'On no account draw near.'

In Jesus' day Jewish people had the strongest inbuilt reasons for narrowness of sympathy. And the liberation brought by Jesus – and more widely, by some of his early followers, like Paul the Apostle – was a remarkable development, often imperfectly sustained. Of course, we cannot realistically feel at home with all kinds of people equally, however free we are from inbuilt prejudice: we are shy and tongue-tied with those who are very different and where we do not know how to break through. Those are weaknesses to be candid about and we go wrong when we turn them into principles. God is Father of us all and the coming of Jesus broke through to us all.

- Pray for resolution to widen our sympathies.
- Thank God for the universal gift of light.

ANNUNCIATION OF OUR LORD TO THE BLESSED VIRGIN MARY (25 MARCH)

THE BLESSED VIRGIN MARY (15 AUGUST)

LUKE 1.26–38

In the sixth month the angel Gabriel was sent by God to a town in Galilee called Nazareth, to a virgin engaged to a man whose name was Joseph, of the house of David. The virgin's name was Mary.

And he came to her and said, 'Greetings, favoured one! The Lord is with you.'

But she was much perplexed by his words and pondered what sort of greeting this might be.

The angel said to her, 'Do not be afraid, Mary, for you have found favour with God. And now, you will conceive in your womb and bear a son, and you will name him Jesus. He will be great, and will be called the Son of the Most High, and the Lord God will give to him the throne of his ancestor David.

'He will reign over the house of Jacob for ever, and of his kingdom there will be no end.'

Mary said to the angel, 'How can this be, since I am a virgin?'

The angel said to her, 'The Holy Spirit will come upon you, and the power of the Most High will overshadow you; therefore the child to be born will be holy; he will be called Son of God.

'And now, your relative Elizabeth in her old age has also conceived a son; and this is the sixth month for her who was said to be barren. For nothing will be impossible with God.'

Then Mary said, 'Here am I, the servant of the Lord; let it be with me according to your word.' Then the angel departed from her.

COMMENTARY

The story gives us the beginning of the coming of Jesus among us. As Christians, we believe that in him we receive our clearest and most direct picture of God. He is our best route to him. Endless paintings have depicted the moving, simple encounter between God and the human race, with Gabriel and Mary as representative. So Mary is both herself and our stand-in. The simple, humble acceptance that Mary shows is for us to show too – that Christ may be born in us and God's will be done in the world. But though the lesson for us is clear and true, we need to reflect keenly on the scene before us, in order to be taken out of ourselves and to absorb the simplicity of Mary.

REFLECTION

The feasts of Mary are also feasts of Jesus for she is nowhere without him. We see her depicted as placing herself in that humble role: the willing agent of God's purposes.

It is a tragedy that, for many, she has become, over a long period, a figure of conflict, even hatred. In large parts of Christianity anything approaching devotion to her or loving regard for her is rejected. In other parts, it sometimes *seems* that she is a figure of faith and devotion in what looks like her own right. For centuries, such devotion has been central to Catholic Christians. Historically, this arose at a time when Jesus seemed so lofty a figure that it did not feel proper for mere sinful mortals to approach him directly, whereas Mary could a bit more easily be seen as 'one of us'. Today, it is good to set aside these extremes and to see Mary as Luke, chiefly, depicted her in his Gospel: as the willing receiver of grace and the ready agent of God's great purpose. However, she helps to show us that there's never any ground for giving anything but the highest values to all humans – and she can stand as our standard-bearer.

- Pray to receive Mary with love and thanks.

- Pray to be spared from the quarrels and distortions that can warp our prayers.

TRANSFIGURATION OF OUR LORD (6 AUGUST)

MARK 9.2-8

Six days later, Jesus took with him Peter and James and John, and led them up a high mountain apart, by themselves. And he was transfigured before them, and his clothes became dazzling white, such as no one on earth could bleach them.

And there appeared to them Elijah with Moses, who were talking with Jesus.

Then Peter said to Jesus, 'Rabbi, it is good for us to be here; let us make three dwellings, one for you, one for Moses, and one for Elijah.' He did not know what to say, for they were terrified.

Then a cloud overshadowed them, and from the cloud there came a voice, 'This is my Son, the Beloved; listen to him!'

Suddenly when they looked around, they saw no one with them any more, but only Jesus.

COMMENTARY

The theme of Christ the King is not without its complications. Popular hymns take it in their stride, and so do the language of devotion and the conventions of Christian art. The aim of today's celebration is of course to enforce the message that Christians place the authority of Christ – what he stood for and what he asks of us – above all other powers to which we may be subject. *Their* claims often seem to dominate life, in some societies more than others, but the authority of Christ has the sanction of our creator and our ultimate Lord, God himself. The story of the Transfiguration of Jesus in the presence of his disciples is designed to assure us that, despite all normal appearances and despite the Cross that begins to loom, Jesus' authority is supreme and inviolable. He is greater than even the great ones of old Israel who brought God's older guidance to his people.

REFLECTION

Current British attitudes to authority are so complex as to discourage analysis. Many people have little respect for traditional authorities and keep out of their way as much as they possibly can. A good many, including those in this first category, complain with vigour about alleged authorities while at the same time doing everything possible to frustrate their proper activities. At the personal level, therapists will often make a bee-line for authority figures and the impression they made, including their long-term legacy, for good or ill, whether parents, teachers or even partners – let alone employers, dominant friends and figures in churches.

But what about God as an authority figure? At first sight, it's straightforward. If we believe in him seriously, then is he not the greatest authority of all? There is no evading him, surely; and may not he be as destructive for us as perhaps people in our families have been? For few of us are wholly unscathed. Then we attend to Jesus: vulnerable, and in life and death, powerless. He then can mature us, for he does not – cannot – threaten us. And we learn that the path of simple love is the key: no strident assertion, or even quiet defensive barrier-building; neither any passive acquiescence in things as they are. Open love will show us both ourselves and God.

- Pray for the maturing influence of love.
- Pray for those who exercise authority in your life.
- Pray for those who make decisions over the lives of others.

COMMEMORATION OF ALL SOULS (2 NOVEMBER)

WISDOM OF SOLOMON 3.1-9

But the souls of the righteous are in the hands of God, and no torment will ever touch them. In the eyes of the foolish they seemed to have died, and their departure was thought to be a disaster, and their going from us to be their destruction: but they are at peace.

For though in the sight of others they were punished, their hope is full of immortality. Having been disciplined a little, they will receive great good, because God tested them and found them worthy of himself; like gold in the furnace he tried them, and like a sacrificial burnt-offering he accepted them.

In the time of their visitation they will shine forth, and will run like sparks through the stubble. They will govern nations and rule over peoples, and the Lord will reign over them for ever.

Those who trust in him will understand truth.

COMMENTARY

We read the Old Testament in vain for teaching on life beyond the grave. But now, in the Wisdom of Solomon, probably written close to the time of Jesus, we have important Jewish teaching on this subject. In our day, as so often in the past and for people of many faiths, it is a matter of great concern to many. The passage meets this concern with hope and confidence – in God and his good purpose for his people. Christians go further and relate our hope to Jesus, focusing on his resurrection and our union with him through our baptism and through our faithfulness of life here and now. So we pray for the departed, not in a spirit of fret or hopeless demand, but in a spirit of assurance based on our unity in Christ.

REFLECTION

All of us know the power of disease and the sheer fragility of life in the face of death. All Saints' Day gives us the witness to the victory of incarnate goodness and All Souls proclaims our common mortality expressed in our aspirations and expectations of shared eternity. Yet we fear death and we live in a culture that does not enable us to look death in the face: to befriend it.

We also need to hope. Christians dare to hope beyond the constraints of mortality, embodied in saints and souls, a vast company and communion dwelling beyond time and for ever.

That is why we need this day. We know how hard and unpredictable life is. We know how difficult it is to say goodbye to those we have loved and let them rest in the peace of God's eternity. We should see the flickering light of life's vitality in the face of one another and trust all life and death to the source of creation.

The limitations of our understanding and obstacles of time may redirect the springs of eternal life to the arid landscape of our hopelessness. Let us allow this relentless and irrepressible stream of living water to find its way to the desert around us, and through us to all we love.

- Pray that God will embrace all living and departed with his forgiving love.

- Give thanks for those loved ones who have shaped our lives for good.

- How would you like to be remembered?

REMEMBRANCE SUNDAY

REVELATION 21.1–6

Then I saw a new heaven and a new earth; for the first heaven and the first earth had passed away, and the sea was no more. And I saw the holy city, the new Jerusalem, coming down out of heaven from God, prepared as a bride adorned for her husband. And I heard a loud voice from the throne saying,

'See, the home of God is among mortals. He will dwell with them; they will be his peoples, and God himself will be there with them; he will wipe every tear from their eyes. Death will be no more; mourning and crying and pain will be no more, for the first things have passed away.'

And the one who was seated on the throne said, 'See, I am making all things new.'

Also he said, 'Write this, for these words are trustworthy and true.'

Then he said to me, 'It is done! I am the Alpha and the Omega, the beginning and the end. To the thirsty I will give water as a gift from the spring of the water of life.'

COMMENTARY

Violent death has always had a special place in people's hearts and in their prayerful memories – look at the effigies of medieval knights in many of our churches. But in the past century, in effect since 1914, the scale of warfare has changed and, with its huge cost in lives, mostly not old-style professional soldiers but ordinary citizens, volunteers or conscripts, the intensity of 'remembrance' has changed to match. It is no wonder that in the countries most affected, the allotted day continues to be observed widely and devoutly. It is good that the day should be kept also with hope and resolve for a better future. So we widen our vision and share that of the Revelation of John for the time of universal peace and love. The world and life within it seem to lack meaning if God will not bring it to peace and perfection. And the love of God must be at the heart for all of us.

REFLECTION

From time to time, the Remembrance Day observance has given rise to a certain amount of disquiet among Christian people, as well as among others. In markedly peaceful times, it comes to seem morbid or else jingoistic to maintain the ceremonies associated with this time. Yet they do make us all too aware of renewed warfare, even involving our own country. Whether we approve or deplore, the solemn and tragic facts speak for themselves.

Others feel that for the purity of Christian witness it is undesirable to muddy the waters by mixing religious faith with secular affairs, however tragic or solemn. But there is another Christian way of looking at the matter. And this has more body to it, even if it can degenerate into a selling of the Christian soul to the powers that be – which has a history, sometimes ghastly, in many lands. Try this: God gives us the whole setting of our lives; not just the Church, not just the Christian religion, but the whole picture – and all is his gift. So Christians must resist immorality in civic life, including immoral wars, but we play our part in all aspects of the society we live in, and where necessary we get our hands dirty on behalf of God.

- Pray for our native land and for the purifying of its life.
- Remember all who have died in war, and who work for peace.

CREATION/HARVEST/
ROGATION (EASTER 6)
ONE WORLD WEEK

PSALM 19.1–6

The heavens are telling the glory of God; and the firmament proclaims his handiwork. Day to day pours forth speech, and night to night declares knowledge.

There is no speech, nor are there words; their voice is not heard: yet their voice goes out through all the earth, and their words to the end of the world.

In the heavens he has set a tent for the sun, which comes out like a bridegroom from his wedding canopy, and like a strong man runs its course with joy. Its rising is from the end of the heavens, and its circuit to the end of them; and nothing is hidden from its heat.

COMMENTARY

The Old Testament is better than the New at making us see the greatness and the wonder of God's creation. The psalm is just one example. Whether we are seeking to deepen our sense of the world we all inhabit, to grow in our duty of responsibility for the welfare of all within it, both human and material, or to give thanks at harvest for its role in sustaining our life, the message is the same. We respond to God with wonder and gratitude for the world in which we are placed – and for which we are stewards. The misuse of the natural order by many humans and its appalling effects in poverty and disease reduce us to humble silence, but also, surely, to a resolve to link ourselves more closely to God's will for the good of all.

REFLECTION

More than ever before, wherever we live, we feel ourselves to be all of one world – dependent on each other, rich when others are rich, threatened with ills that afflict them – even though gross inequalities remain. We know, even if we fail to act on it, that we are our fellows' keeper, weeping with those who weep and rejoicing with those who rejoice.

All this brings home to us, more than ever before, the one created order that we all share and of which God chooses to make us responsible tenants. This is then not simply the reminder of creative acts of long ago, but the recognition of the present order. Moreover, it directs us to renewed vision of the world's destiny, as a perfected order must emerge, to which we shall have contributed. So the image is not one of a static world order, but of a dynamic creation in which we are privileged to share, for the glory of the one creator of all.

- Pray for the right use of the world's resources.

- We are to recognize humbly our true role in the order and destiny of the earth.

CREATION/HARVEST
ONE WORLD WEEK

REVELATION 22.1–5

Then the angel showed me the river of the water of life, bright as crystal, flowing from the throne of God and of the Lamb through the middle of the street of the city.

On either side of the river is the tree of life with its twelve kinds of fruit, producing its fruit each month: and the leaves of the tree are for the healing of the nations.

Nothing accursed will be found there any more. But the throne of God and of the Lamb will be in it, and his servants will worship him; they will see his face, and his name will be on their foreheads.

And there will be no more night; they need no light of lamp or sun, for the Lord God will be their light, and they will reign for ever and ever.

COMMENTARY

Shortly before the time of Jesus, and for a while after, some Jewish writers developed a visionary and poetic way of telling their readers about a believer's legitimate hope for the future. The writing is often vivid and, to many modern people, rather weird. Yet it is in part a code of symbols based on profound and confident belief that God will one day make everything good and pure for the world and for his people. Around the end of the first century, John, imprisoned for his faith on the island of Patmos, wrote a book of this character, called by its technical name, 'Apocalypse' or 'Revelation'. Here, near the end, the writer describes his beautiful vision for the world that God created. Its end will be a time of bliss and fulfilment. We note that the garden which was the paradise in Genesis is now a city, full of people, blessed by God. Everything will at last be in unity, peace and perfection. It is a hope to cherish and not to allow to fade.

REFLECTION

Farmers know from the inside what we should all know from the outside – that we should never take the harvest for granted. We recognize our dependence upon God and the gifts that he gives us through the beauty and wonder of the world around us.

If you break up the single letters of the word 'harvest' they can spell out 'starve' or 'share'. When we pray the Lord's Prayer we say: 'Give us today our daily bread' – we pray always give *us* and not give *me*. God's gifts are for sharing with everyone. It is not God's will that some people should have so much while others scratch and starve. So we cannot keep this festival without remembering the many millions who live in poverty and conditions of perpetual starvation. All that we have comes from God, and we are required to be good stewards and generous with his gifts.

Do we know the difference between obligation and responsibility? Think of your breakfast of bacon and eggs. The chicken was involved and made a contribution whereas the pig gave total commitment! Are we as Christians prepared to make a total commitment to God's creation and our duties and responsibilities as guardians?

• Pray for all those agencies working to make poverty history.

• Give thanks for all those who bring us our food.

SAINTS' DAYS

MATTHEW 5.1–12

When Jesus saw the crowds, he went up the mountain; and after he sat down, his disciples came to him. Then he began to speak, and taught them, saying:

'Blessed are the poor in spirit, for theirs is the kingdom of heaven.

'Blessed are those who mourn, for they will be comforted.

'Blessed are the meek, for they will inherit the earth.

'Blessed are those who hunger and thirst for righteousness, for they will be filled.

'Blessed are the merciful, for they will receive mercy.

'Blessed are the pure in heart, for they will see God.

'Blessed are the peacemakers, for they will be called children of God.

'Blessed are those who are persecuted for righteousness' sake, for theirs is the kingdom of heaven.

'Blessed are you when people revile you and persecute you and utter all kinds of evil against you falsely on my account.

'Rejoice and be glad, for your reward is great in heaven, for in the same way they persecuted the prophets who were before you.'

COMMENTARY

The eight beatitudes open the Sermon on the Mount, the great core of Jesus' teaching as given in the Gospel of Matthew (5–7). The subject is life in the Kingdom of God which Jesus comes to proclaim. In these brief statements, we see outlined the key features of the Christian character. Those who attain this style of life, with those preferences to the fore in both mind and deed, will certainly receive God's 'blessing' – the seal and endorsement of his love. The first of the eight is perhaps the hardest to understand: one attempt to be clearer said, 'Blessed are those who know their need of God' – that is, who can abandon all pride and pretence before God. We may see this as basic to all the other qualities and courses of life that we are to pursue.

REFLECTION

In the saints we have no roll-call of past heroes but rather they are our sisters and brothers; they are with us on the way, alongside as companions and guides, sustaining us with their prayers and guiding us by their example. Perhaps we need to be liberated from a dull, pedestrian, bureaucratic, utilitarian view of the Church which is hardly likely to inspire anyone!

The saints through their rich and diverse witness help us to recover a vision of the Church which is God's and not ours. Here we recognize readily the brokenness and sinfulness of humanity, knowing our need of God yet at the same time rejoicing in the abundant mercy and grace of God who in Christ comes to us.

One of the ways in which the saints are honoured is their search for God. They have immersed themselves in Scripture, prayer and service. They challenge us to an adventure: a quest and search for truth that enlightens our path and fires our imaginations.

So let us seek to ground and inform ourselves in the way of God. Let us try to look beyond our own assumptions and limitations to see things whole – full-face to God and to each other, with all the excitement and risk that that involves.

- Give thanks for all those saints who offer us an example of discipleship.

- May God enrich our imaginations to discover new depths of understanding.

- Spend time to know God.

THE LEVESON CENTRE FOR THE STUDY OF AGEING, SPIRITUALITY AND SOCIAL POLICY

What is the Leveson Centre?

The Leveson Centre for the Study of Ageing, Spirituality and Social Policy, part of The Foundation of Lady Katherine Leveson at Temple Balsall near Solihull, was launched in January 2001 to be a local and national focus for practical education, training, research and reflection on the role of older people in the twenty-first century.

What are our aims?

Inspired by the belief that older people should not be considered passive recipients of care, but valued and cherished as members of society who can inform and enrich the lives of others:

- we are a focus for interdisciplinary study of ageing, spirituality and social policy
- we establish and make accessible information about these subjects
- we contribute to best practice through publications, conferences, public lectures and seminars
- we network with other agencies, projects and individuals
- we are developing an understanding of spirituality as lived by older people, and support them to express their spiritual awareness – and learn from them
- we support and enable older people to influence policy makers, professionals, carers and churches
- we identify and disseminate distinctive contributions that Christian churches can make to the development of social policy and see how we may bridge gaps between theory and practice
- we explore multicultural aspects of ageing and welcome people of all faiths – and none
- we sponsor or coordinate research projects.

What are our main activities?

We have run a series of successful seminars on a variety of topics, including quality of life for people with dementia, palliative care and dementia, worship with older people, long-term care, spiritual pain, caring for carers, the spiritual needs of older people, a good funeral, learning in later life, and culture, faith and old age. We have also organized three research symposiums, bringing together people from related disciplines to share their work. We produce a newsletter (currently twice a year) which, together with specially commissioned articles, includes information about the Centre, news of policy initiatives concerned with ageing, details of other related projects, forthcoming events and notices, and reviews of recently published books.

For details as they become available, please see our website